We All
We Got

PITT
BASKETBALL
IN THE
GOLDEN ERA

Printed in the United States of America.

ISBN: 978-1-59571-350-6

Library of Congress Control Number: 2008943820

Designed and published by:

Word Association Publishers
205 Fifth Avenue
Tarentum, Pennsylvania 15084
www.wordassociation.com
1-800-827-7903

All photographs courtesy of the University of Pittsburgh Department of Athletics.

We All We Got

PITT
BASKETBALL
IN THE
GOLDEN ERA

MICHAEL E. LOWENSTEIN

FOREWORD BY:
MARK A. NORDENBERG
CHANCELLOR
UNIVERSITY OF PITTSBURGH

DEDICATION

As I went through my Pitt basketball message board "posts" of the past seven years, I was reminded of the old joke of one of those folksy Southern coaches, Abe Lemons or somebody, about the player who comes into the coach's office to ask what he should do about his grades, which were four Fs and a D:

"Son, I think you are spending too much time on that one subject."

****

Still, as I looked back over them, I thought there was something there, something we had experienced. So I set about to edit some of the posts I liked the best, to make them shorter—which at times you will find hard to believe—and a little more readable. Or to see if I could make a point a little better than I made it at the time. I believe I have retained the essence of these posts and certainly tried to do so.

I have added some comments in italics before each post, and occasionally inside a post, to provide context. For the same reason, I included the dates and scores of some of the games, not all of them, but the ones that I felt were most important.

****

I struggled over the title for months. It finally came to me right after I finished the first draft. "We All We Got" was a slogan of the 2003-2004 Pitt Panther basketball team. Many "educated" people I know would throw that back at me as an example of the kind of kids Pitt had playing basketball, the kind they would never have at "their" schools.

To me it was pure and it was perfect, from the first time I heard it. I have special memories of a trip to New Jersey that spring to see Pitt in the Sweet 16, a trip where my father took us to see his parents' graves outside Newark, me for the first time since my grandmother died in 1980, and him maybe for the last time, and then we all went back—my parents, my family, and my sister down from Boston and her family—and put on our "We All We Got" shirts and went to watch Pitt play Oklahoma State.

When I told my wife that I was putting these posts into a book, and that this is what I had been doing in the basement all this time, she laughed and rolled her eyes. I told her that I had a title and she laughed and rolled her eyes again and said, "Let's hear it." I told her, and she paused, and she stopped rolling her eyes and she said, "That's good…That really is good."

This is for my family. We all we got.

FOREWORD

In March of 2003, I attended the first and second round games of the NCAA men's basketball tournament in Boston. It was a terrific weekend for University of Pittsburgh fans. Our Panthers beat Wagner by 26 points in their first round game and completed their run through the bracket with a decisive 22-point win over the Indiana Hoosiers, a traditional basketball power.

While walking through a Fleet Center concourse on the night of the Wagner game, I had a chance meeting with my long-time friend Martha Munsch. More than twenty-five years earlier, Martha and I had occupied offices next to each other while serving as young members of the Pitt law faculty. Even after she left the academic life to return to private practice, I enjoyed regular contact with Martha, who did legal work for the University and later served as a Pitt Trustee.

There is another side to Martha that I also came to know quite well. As an undergraduate student, she was the first woman to serve as sports editor of *The Pitt News.* And as a young mother, she reportedly named her son "Dan" in honor of legendary Panther quarterback Dan Marino. As those bits of history suggest, at every stage of her life, Martha has been one of Pitt's most knowledgeable and passionate fans.

When Martha first asked, in that concourse conversation, if I knew her law firm partner Mike Lowenstein, who also was attending the tournament, I attached no particular significance to the question. However, her follow-up caught my attention. "You are not going to believe Mike," she exclaimed, "because you have never met a more committed Pitt fan!" Frankly, I thought that I had been exposed to the ultimate in fan loyalty through my exposure to Martha herself and was not sure if I should consider her description of Mike to be welcoming or a warning.

Before long, though, I had the chance to judge for myself. I not only met Mike but worked closely with him. During our "time of troubles" with the ACC, Mike served as a lead litigator for the Big East Conference. As a client who also has been a lawyer, a law professor and a law school dean, I can report that he did a fabulous job. I quickly came to respect him as a professional, to like him as a person—and, as Martha Munsch had predicted, to be amazed by his level of commitment as a fan.

To put that statement in proper context, let me make clear that Mike possesses none of the negative qualities that frame stereotypes of the uncontrollably rabid fan. He understands that college athletes are moving through a period of personal growth and extends to them a suitable measure of patience. He realizes that most coaches actually do know more than he does—about their sport and about their team—and is willing to give them some benefit of the doubt even when he disagrees with their decisions. And he knows how to accept a loss with dignity, whatever internal pain it may have brought to him.

The book that Mike has written chronicles what he has labeled the "Golden Era" of Pitt basketball. It is an era that began earlier in this decade and that continues today. It is an era that has unfolded in a spectacular new facility, the John M. and Gertrude E. Peterson Events Center. It is an era that was shaped by two outstanding coaches, Jamie Dixon and Ben Howland. And it is an era that was built by committed players, whose hard-work and team-first approach enabled them to triumph with a level of consistency that has been among the best in the country and that exceeded even their considerable talent levels.

It also is an era that has brought great pleasure to a large number of fans. Some of them—like Martha Munsch, Michael Lowenstein and Mark Nordenberg—had lived loyally through many earlier seasons when championships seemed out of reach. Others were comparatively new to Pitt basketball and had been given a first opportunity to follow the team when the construction of the Peterson Center virtually doubled the number of seats available on game-day.

Today, that large fan base probably is best known for "the Oakland Zoo," the students who have helped make being at "the Pete" more joyful for the Panthers, more challenging for their opponents and more fun for everyone else. The crowds also include more mature individuals—faculty, staff and alumni from Pitt, as well as fans from the broader community. And, of course, that fan base extends to families who follow the fortunes of the Panthers together. Among these families are the Lowensteins.

This book, then, also is their story—a story of bonding through basketball. Theirs is a family that not only attends almost every home game but travels to many away games. It is a family that seems to understand when Mike, who already has seen a game in person, invests further time in watching recorded replays. It is a family that has found joy in sharing the Pitt basketball experience with each other, and I am very glad that Mike has made the effort, through this book, to share that experience with others as well.

Mark A. Nordenberg
Chancellor
University of Pittsburgh
January 2009

PROLOGUE

Basketball was a new game in the 20th century and the University of Pittsburgh played it like everybody else. But most of the time they did not play it very well.

There was, I'm told, a great run in the late 1920s with three-time All-American Charles Hyatt and Coach Doc Carlson, at a time when there was a jump ball after every basket. A Final Four team in 1941, even if there were only eight teams in the tournament. In the 1950s, a wonderful little guard from Wampum, Pennsylvania named Don Hennon, who once made the same All-American team as Wilt Chamberlain, Oscar Robertson and Elgin Baylor.

Many years later, in 1974, my senior year of high school, an honest-to-goodness terrific Pitt team, one that won 22 games in a row led by future NBA All-Star Billy Knight and the invention of something called the "amoeba defense." That Pitt team reached the regional finals, much later known as the Elite Eight. There they played N.C. State in a game best known for the great David Thompson jumping so high that he hit his foot on the shoulder of his 6-8 N.C. State teammate Phil Spence. Thompson landed on his head with such a hollow thud that everyone in the arena and watching on television gasped at the possibility that the best college basketball player in the country had just died on the court. By the time he returned from the hospital to the bench, to the relief of all, his head swathed in bandages, an inspired N.C. State had broken open a close game. They went on to win the national championship.

A few other pretty good teams and some fine players, and that was about it for the first 80 years of Pitt basketball. Then, in the early 1980s, at a time when Pitt was riding a wave of national prominence in football, Pitt joined the Big East basketball conference and made a serious effort to energize its long-middling basketball program.

It began with a small parade of what were then known as "High School All-Americans," starting in 1983 with Curtis Aiken from Buffalo. A year later, Demetreus Gore arrived from Detroit, along with the signature recruit of the era, 6-10 Charles Smith of Bridgeport, Connecticut, who would make All-American and play on the Olympic team before a long NBA career. The next year, one more, perhaps the most memorable. Jerome Lane, from Akron St. Vincent-St. Mary's, the school that, many years later, would produce Lebron James. Jerome Lane came to Pitt hoping to play point guard and ended up leading the country in rebounding. He once explained that he might as well rebound since he was under the basket anyway. Lane still is fondly recalled in basketball circles for the night he sailed in from the right wing and threw one down with such force that he shattered the backboard, an event also remembered for Bill Raftery's famous call of "Send it in Jerome!"

It took awhile for them to grow up, and it took a toll on Coach

Roy Chipman, who left in 1986. Paul Evans came over from Navy, where his team, led by David Robinson, had just reached the Elite Eight. The Evans era began well. After a 15-14 record in Chipman's last year, Pitt shot up to the top of the Big East. In Evans's second year, 1987-88, Pitt won the Big East regular season championship, its first ever, on my 31st birthday, when Lane had 29 points and 15 rebounds in the Carrier Dome against Syracuse star and future first pick in the NBA draft, Derrick Coleman.

Pitt entered the NCAA Tournament that year as a Number 2 seed, handled Eastern Michigan in Lincoln, Nebraska and, after a struggle, it appeared they would get past a good Vanderbilt team in the second round. Vanderbilt was fouling and shooting three-pointers to try and catch up, but Pitt was making most of their foul shots. Vanderbilt still trailed by three points with only seconds to play. With a win, Pitt would play Kansas, a team which, according to its own coach, Larry Brown, did not match up with Pitt at all.

Here, the facts get murky. Afterward, Paul Evans would claim that he told the Pitt players to foul Vanderbilt before they could shoot a tying three-pointer. Lane later said that Evans did not call for a foul but that his young assistant, John Calipari, did. Whatever did or did not happen in that huddle, what happened on the court was clear enough: Pitt did not foul, Vanderbilt's best outside shooter, Barry Goheen, hit a desperation three-pointer, the game went to overtime, Vanderbilt won, Kansas won the national championship, Smith and Lane went pro and the Pitt program slid downhill for almost 15 years.

For a generation, there have been two things to say to stop any Pitt fan cold. The first is "48-14," the score by which hated rival Penn State upset an undefeated and Number 1-ranked Pitt football team led by Dan Marino in 1981. The second is "Barry Goheen." Both have been said to me many times.

By the fall of 1994, Paul Evans was gone, followed by Ralph Willard, a successful coach before he came to Pitt and after he left, but who did not succeed at Pitt. In 1999, Pitt tried again, this time with a little-known coach from Northern Arizona, Ben Howland.

****

In April 2008, after defeating Ben Howland's UCLA team in the Final Four, Memphis was in the process of losing a nine-point lead in the last two minutes and twelve seconds against Kansas in the national championship game. Memphis still led by three in the final seconds, when a magnificent freshman guard named Derrick Rose, already perhaps the best player in the country, failed to foul a Kansas player. This allowed Kansas's Mario Chalmers to hit a miracle three-pointer to force overtime, after which Kansas pulled away to win the championship, just as it had twenty years earlier. The Memphis coach was John Calipari. Within minutes, a friend emailed: "Somewhere in America tonight, Barry Goheen smiled and

Paul Evans allowed himself a wry chuckle." Calipari did remember to take the blame, whether it was his or not.

****

As history was repeating itself for John Calipari and Kansas, I was putting the finishing touches on a book about a different era in Pitt basketball. An era that is continuing and one that we will look back on, unquestionably, as the Golden Era in Pitt Basketball. A time when Pitt played basketball the way it was meant to be played, not for a season or two, but for years and years.

I was ready to complete this book and send it out into the world. But not without hesitation. I am known as well past normal on the subject of Pitt basketball. This book would confirm that beyond doubt. I knew what I wanted to do, in truth what I had to do, but I needed a sign.

****

In my spare time I am a workaday lawyer and have been these past 28 years. The Sunday following the Memphis-Kansas national championship game in 2008 I went to the Pitt basketball banquet, a feel-good affair to celebrate the end of the college basketball season. Teams all over the country have them. When I got home, I checked my computer. A co-defendant had hired a prominent Atlanta law firm on a new case in which I had just gotten involved. There was an email from a partner at this firm, someone with whom I had never dealt before.

It was from Barry Goheen.

CHAPTER ONE

THE FIRST TIME

By December 19, 2001, its brief stab at college basketball glory a distant memory, Pitt had long since become an afterthought in the Big East Conference, with an unbroken string of forgettable basketball seasons:

1993-1994	13-14
1994-1995	10-18
1995-1996	10-17
1996-1997	18-15
1997-1998	11-16
1998-1999	14-16
1999-1000	13-15
2000-2001	19-14

To us, though, it was our team, and it always had been. Our three children were teenagers, the youngest, our son, born three months after the Pitt-Vanderbilt game of 1988. Since they were old enough to remember, they had never seen one really good Pitt basketball team. Not one. We always believed it was about to change.

****

The 2001-2002 season was supposed to be more of the same. The Big East coaches picked Pitt to finish sixth in what was then known, somewhat anomalously, as the West division of the Big East. Out of seven. Instead, Pitt finished ninth.

In the country.

Basketball as it was meant to be played. By *our* team.

Finally.

****

My 13-year-old son and I had suspected it when we headed up Cardiac Hill on the Pitt campus in November 2001 to see the annual Blue-Gold intra-squad scrimmage at the old Pitt Field House. The Field House was right next to where they were building the Peterson Center, or, as it became known, the Pete, the new arena for which Chancellor Mark Nordenberg and Athletic Director Steve Pederson had fought because they knew Pitt urgently needed it to have a chance to compete. On the surface, this Pitt team looked like Pitt teams had looked for a long time. A bunch of decent players. Just not the thoroughbreds the big teams had.

But this Pitt team had a leader at point guard, the most important position. Brandin Knight, the lightly-recruited younger brother of NBA player Brevin Knight, had been passed over by Seton Hall, his hometown school where his father had played and coached. From the day he got here, we knew that Brandin Knight was a basketball genius. I would tell my friend Jim, one of the few real basketball fans in Pittsburgh then: "I can't explain to you how good this kid can be, what he can see on the court, the instincts, the sense of pace." Brandin had a lot of growing up to do, physically, and, by some accounts, in other ways. "At the beginning, Brandin did not always like to practice," or words to that effect. The growing up had started to happen at the end of the previous year, when, after only six wins in the Big East tournament in 18 years, Brandin and the departed Ricky Greer led Pitt to the finals, something the Big East coaches had overlooked when they picked Pitt for the bottom of the league again that fall.

Brandin was a junior. Julius Page, a sophomore from Buffalo, returned at shooting guard after having started as a freshman. Julius had enjoyed his SportsCenter moment the previous winter when, at maybe 6-2, he dunked right in the face of 7-0 Ruben Boumtje Boumtje of Georgetown on a snowy night in January when Pitt had gone down to Georgetown and beaten a 16-0 Georgetown team—something else the experts had skipped past that fall. Julius played center in high school and his ball-handling and shooting were works in progress. But he was a great defender and he could jump so high and with such confidence that Brandin used to throw him lob passes, as Brandin once explained, just to shut him up.

There were two 6-7, 235-pound kids. Donatas Zavackas, a junior from Lithuania, was an interesting strain of European player. He had the usual things: smart, good shooter, a good floor game. But he also had a nasty streak. We called him Rocky V. Actually, he was nasty pretty much all the time, and he could defend the post, even though he couldn't jump, not even a little, and he couldn't run much either. Chevy Troutman, a redshirt freshman from Williamsport, PA could run, he could jump and he could rebound. Pitt recruited Chevy to play the small forward but he couldn't, at least not yet. At the start he couldn't shoot beyond two feet from the hoop. It took the coaches half the season to realize that he didn't need to.

A couple of roly-poly guys: Jaron Brown, a redshirt sophomore from Lexington, Kentucky; and Ontario Lett, who had been out of organized basketball. Of Lett, Ben Howland once said, "Sometimes you have to get lucky in this business." Pitt found Lett somewhere in Florida in the middle of the previous summer and offered him a scholarship on a playground after assistant coach Jamie Dixon noticed that his wingspan was 86 inches or something. Eight months later he was on the Big East All-Tournament team. Lett was listed at 6-6. I once heard Howland say that he was 6-4 and a half. Either way, Lett had a classic college post game: 270 pounds, easy, with great hands and feet. He played with a big smile on his face and it took about a half-hour to get around him.

Jaron. A lefty, like Julius. As unlikely-looking a basketball player as you will ever see. The year he sat out I swear he was 6-2, 250. As calm a soul as you would ever hope to see, too. Even now, when he's been gone four seasons, I watch the tapes and I am still learning about the things Jaron Brown could do on a basketball court. How he could guard four positions.

How he knew the game. How he made people better.

To this day, we have never replaced Jaron. Even more than Brandin. Because, at that scrimmage in 2001, Carl was there too, even though he was sitting out and it was the only time we would see him play that season. Carl Krauser, as he would let the world know, from the Bronx. Even if Carl Krauser never fully replaced Brandin Knight on the court or in our hearts, and even though my son and I fought about Carl for three years and whether it was OK that he wasn't Brandin, we still had Carl. But we have never replaced Jaron.

Chad Johnson, a transfer from Nebraska, was the only senior and the captain. 6-5 and lean, and a good defender, Johnson was the son of former NBA power forward Clemon Johnson. Sophomore Torrie Morris was a 6-11, 280 project from Tennessee who worked hard and got better, so much better that, after a college career as a part-time player, he was the last cut on an NBA team one season. Finally, a couple of redshirt freshmen: Mark McCarroll, 6-10, about 200, childhood friend in New York of rapper 50 Cent, and Yuri Demetris, a 6-3 guard, who despite his name was the only scholarship player on the whole team from Pittsburgh. Western Pennsylvania basketball had fallen far from the days of Maurice Stokes and Don Hennon and Norm Van Lier and Kenny Durrett and Maurice Lucas and Billy Knight and George Karl and Mickey and Brad Davis. And Ricky Coleman, who was the star of Lucas's high school team, the legendary Schenley High team of 1971—a team that, when I was in ninth grade, came to our school and scored 151 points in a 32-minute game—and who, if he hadn't gotten hurt, might have been better than all of them.

So there it was, the 2001-02 Pitt Panthers. On the surface, just a bunch of modestly recruited players from all over the place. The kind of players who get you picked sixth in the West division of the Big East. The kind of players you find on a hundred teams.

Still, at the Blue-Gold scrimmage that night, we suspected that something was different. Ben Howland, hired by Steve Pederson and Chancellor Nordenberg in 1999, now had his system in place. His team had heeded his direction that they needed to get stronger if they wanted to compete in the Big East. They had a leader in Brandin Knight. They moved the ball. And they had something else, something that was so foreign to almost all of the Pitt teams I had watched for over 30 years, even the few good ones, that it took me a while to figure out that it was called defense.

****

Until December 19, 2001 we only suspected…

That night, Pitt traveled to Columbus to play an Ohio State team that ended up as co-champions of the Big Ten. It was not on television, so we all listened together in the den. Sometimes you can tell what's happening in a basketball game better on the radio anyway. Pitt fell behind early, and caught up by halftime. I took a transistor radio and went for a walk. Pitt fell behind again, and then caught up again with about nine minutes to play. We had seen this movie many times. This is when an OK team playing a good team on the road decides that it has not embarrassed itself and that it is time to lose.

Except that this Pitt team didn't do that. Instead, this Pitt team kept fighting, one grinding, excruciating half-court possession at a time, and then it pulled away, 62-55. It's probably not the best thing for a 44-year-old man to pump his fist and scream out "YES!!" in the middle of a cold December night, like Dennis Hopper at the end of *Hoosiers*.

Because I knew.

****

When I got home, my family did too.

Anything you share with your family is a good thing. I have shared all of this with a very patient wife and our three wonderful children, two daughters and then a son. This helped to justify the time I had started to spend "talking" to other Pitt fans on the "Pantherlair" internet message board which we sometimes still call by (I think) the original name: The Pitt Sports Message Board, or just "the Board."

I chose "17-15" for my "name." That was the score of the first Pitt football game I ever attended, against Notre Dame on November 7, 1964. I went with my father and grandfather. Notre Dame was Number 1 in the country; Pitt would finish 3-5-2. But Pitt fought Notre Dame all that day until they were stopped on a fourth and one in Notre Dame territory late in the game before losing, 17-15. I often have wondered whether there was something about that game at age seven, some cathexis, that made me a Pitt football and basketball fan for life—long after I had lost just about all interest in pro football and pro basketball and a lot of other things. So 17-15 it was, and I started to have conversations with the people my older daughter came to call my imaginary friends—DT and B Man and Midnight Blue and NTOP and Jeffburgh and many others, none of whom, to this day, I ever have spoken to or met.

On the Pitt board, there have been some fascinating people I never would have encountered, a lot of well-intentioned people, and a fair number of people whose mission in life is to find things to complain about and people to blame.

After the Ohio State game, I went online to announce to my new friends that things had changed and that, for the first time since the 1980s, the first time in my children's memory, Pitt was really, really good. This time, they had built it the right way, with a foundation, and they were going to be really, really good for a long time.

The following post makes a point that sounds pretty bland in retrospect. It wasn't. It was a radical thought at the time. Take a look at what the records had been. In fact, this message still comes up once in a long while. Not by me, I might add.

22-7, At Least   Posted on 12/20/01

This team will struggle just to be an average shooting team and anything but a poor foul-shooting team. There is no "go-to" player. There is no true small forward.

So what.

This is a good basketball team. They are well coached. They have chemistry. They are athletic. They play defense. They are developing mental toughness. Except at point guard, they have enough depth. If Knight stays healthy, and the rest of the team reasonably healthy, I say 22-7 going into the Big East Tournament.

At least.

17-15

JANUARY 2, 2002	PITT 77 ST. JOHN'S 54
JANUARY 5, 2002	PITT 77 @ BOSTON COLLEGE 74
JANUARY 8, 2002	PITT 66 @ RUTGERS 58
JANUARY 12, 2002	NOTRE DAME 56 @ PITT 53
JANUARY 15, 2002	MIAMI 76 PITT 69 (2 OT)
JANUARY 19, 2002	PITT 68 @ GEORGETOWN 67
JANUARY 22, 2002	PITT 72 SYRACUSE 57
JANUARY 26, 2002	PITT 67 GEORGETOWN 56

After impressive wins over St. John's at home, at defending Big East champion Boston College and All-American Troy Bell (ending BC's 25-game home winning streak), and then at the RAC against Rutgers, Pitt hit its first real adversity of the season, with a last-minute loss at home to Notre Dame and a double overtime loss at Miami. But they came back to win at Georgetown in a heart-stopper on a put-back by Jaron Brown in a game that featured the surprise emergence from the bench of a very important player, Chevy Troutman. Pitt then came home to hammer Syracuse and beat a good Georgetown team a second time, this time with surprising ease. Picked for nearly last in the Big East, Pitt was 18-3 and looking at a chance to play two games in Pittsburgh in the NCAA Tournament.

Thoughts Posted on 1/28/02

Unless you are Duke or a very few others, teams just don't go 21 games without really getting rocked once or twice, especially on the road. Maybe it will happen at just the worst time, like the 1971 Penn team that was 28-0 and then lost 90-47 in the regional finals to a Villanova team it already had beaten. It hasn't happened yet.

In the meantime, fate has conspired to create a delicious irony. Even two months ago I never would have imagined that I would be spending time worrying about whether Pitt could get to play in the NCAA Tournament in Pittsburgh. I thought it was a given that teams could not play in their home city. They probably shouldn't be able to. Now, at this very moment when Pitt is really good and the first round is in Pittsburgh, they change the rules to make it possible for the high seeds. When they made this change, Pitt had to be the last team they were thinking about.

17-15

JANUARY 30, 2002	NOTRE DAME 89 PITT 76
FEBRUARY 2, 2002	PITT 71 VILLANOVA 59
FEBRUARY 7, 2002	PITT 70 SETON HALL 65
FEBRUARY 10, 2002	PITT 75 @ SYRACUSE 63

Rocked, indeed. Pitt actually trailed Notre Dame by 28 at the half, and wins over Villanova and Seton Hall at home were only slightly more inspiring. Then, down 14 points with 13 and a half minutes to play, about the time the Pitt basketball season traditionally unraveled, our mucking and grinding half-court Panthers unexpectedly turned on the jets and ran Syracuse straight out of the Carrier Dome, led by soon-to-be All-American Brandin Knight.

Wow!   Posted on 2/11/02

Message boards reveal a lot of narcissism. Here it's all about Pitt. Go to the Syracuse board and the only talk is about Syracuse, and the only debate is whether their highly successful coach of 25 years should be fired or executed.

From the Pitt side, a Big East Player of the Year performance by Knight to pull himself off the deck when it counted after a rough first 25 minutes. Juice off the bench from Chad Johnson. Quiet strength from Jaron Brown. Brown is like a parent out there.

My dream is for Pitt to go back to the Carrier Dome this year. But not to play Syracuse. To the Eastern Regional. To play the best and see exactly how good this Pitt team is.

I want Duke.

17-15

THE FIRST TIME

FEBRUARY 16, 2002	PITT 85 @ WEST VIRGINIA 75
FEBRUARY 21, 2002	PITT 78 RUTGERS 59
FEBRUARY 26, 2002	PITT 73 @ SETON HALL 66 (OT)
MARCH 2, 2002	PITT 92 WEST VIRGINIA 65

Pitt continued its magical season, pounding West Virginia twice and Rutgers, and surviving a tough game at Seton Hall when Zavackas hit a three-pointer to force overtime—a result I got from our son when I called him from London in the middle of the night. That made seven straight wins going into the Big East Tournament and a tie with UConn for the regular season championship at 13-3, Pitt's first since the 1988 team led by Charles Smith and Jerome Lane. The second West Virginia game was the last game ever played at the Fitzgerald Field House, a beat-up old armory where I had been watching basketball since I was nine years old.

The Field House   Posted on 3/4/02

25 and 4. *25 and freakin' 4.* At a time when the children all were home and really into it. We always will remember this season, no matter what happens from this point.

I've been coming to the Field House since my dad took me to the high school doubleheaders in 1966. Some favorites:

· Bo Ellis and the Marquette uniforms he supposedly designed.

· Bruce Atkins coming out with a shaved head when Pitt Duquesne mattered.

27

- Darryl Gissendanner blocking Greg Jones's shot against West Virginia and breaking into the Ali Shuffle.

- Sweet George Allen and his ahead-of-his-time long shorts.

- The night the TV crawl read "Matt Miklasevich leads the Big East in sacks."

- Tiger Paul.

- Beating Georgetown with Patrick Ewing and St. John's with Chris Mullin in Pitt's first year in the Big East.

- Charles Smith's first tip-in, above the square, in the first minute of his first game.

- Jerome Lane. The piece of glass that still hangs in my office.

- My friend's 12-year-old son jumping out of his courtside seat to give Brandin Knight a low five after Brandin threw a perfect pass on the break for a dunk.

On Saturday night, before the ceremony introducing five decades of Pitt basketball players, my son's baseball coach at the Boy's Club, Ken Wagoner, defensive ace on Pitt's 1974 Final Eight team, brought over the great All-American from that team, Billy Knight, so my son could meet him.

The Field House is closed. But the circle is unbroken.

17-15

MARCH 7, 2002	PITT 76 BOSTON COLLEGE 62
	[BIG EAST TOURNAMENT]
MARCH 8, 2002	PITT 76 MIAMI 71
	[BIG EAST TOURNAMENT]
MARCH 9, 2002	UCONN 74 PITT 65 (2 OT)
	[BIG EAST FINALS]
MARCH 15, 2002	PITT 71 CENTRAL CONN. ST. 54
	[NCAA TOURNAMENT]
MARCH 17, 2002	PITT 63 CALIFORNIA 50
	[NCAA TOURNAMENT]
MARCH 21, 2002	KENT STATE 78 PITT 73 (OT)
	[NCAA SWEET 16]

2001-2002 RECORD: 29-6

After the last game at the Field House, Pitt went on a stirring run through the Big East Tournament, only to lose a classic double overtime final to a UConn team led by future NBA stars Caron Butler, Emeka Okafor and Ben Gordon. Ontario Lett was brilliant, scoring 17 points and repeatedly challenging the great shot-blocker, Okafor. Brandin Knight was carried off with a knee injury at the end of regulation. After two heroic three-pointers by Zavackas brought them back in overtime, Knight returned, Willis Reed style, to hit the rim on a half court shot that would have won the game. In the second overtime, with UConn up two, a minute to play and Knight out for good, Taliek Brown hit a 30-foot prayer with one second on the shot clock to break open the game for UConn.

Although those two shots are shown from time to time on ESPN and Classic Sports, my posts from the Big East Tournament, like the broadcasts of the last three minutes of the 1974 N.C. State-Maryland game and the seventh game of the 1960 World Series, appear lost to history. So are the posts about Pitt's two NCAA wins in Pittsburgh, after all, and then their overtime loss in Lexington to a Kent State team led by future NFL All-Pro tight end Antonio Gates right after Duke had lost in shocking fashion to Indiana. We were at all of those games, and while the posts were written on lap-tops, they were not saved, except for the one about the obscenely drunken UConn fan at Madison Square Garden in a Caron Butler jersey, "Mullet Man," who added a really bad memory to that classic game.

As I remember these lost posts, they were devoted to many of the themes that I felt—and still feel—about that season: that it was Pitt's time, which, as I look back on it, it was, even if they came up short in the Big East and the NCAAs; that Brandin Knight was a basketball genius; and that I wanted desperately to see a Pitt team with no future pros take on a Duke team that had six. I still choose to believe that if Duke had beaten Indiana that night in Lexington, Pitt would have found a way to beat Kent State. Then we would have seen.

It has been a wonderful seven years but there is nothing like the first time, especially when it comes out of nowhere and your children are all still home to enjoy it.

CHAPTER TWO

THE MOST
SPECIAL TEAM

DECEMBER 18, 2002:	PITT 69 OHIO STATE 49
DECEMBER 31, 2002:	GEORGIA 79 PITT 67
JANUARY 6, 2003:	PITT 72 NOTRE DAME 55
JANUARY 12, 2003:	PITT 70 @ RUTGERS 63
JANUARY 14, 2003:	PITT 80 @ WEST VIRGINIA 61

With everyone back except Chad Johnson, and a terrific young player in Carl Krauser to replace him, Pitt was a Top 5 team from the start of the 2002-2003 season. After missing a chance on New Year's Eve in Georgia to be Number 1 in the country, Pitt bounced back to beat Notre Dame and went on a nice run, including a third straight double-figure win over Syracuse, a team which, by the way, won the national championship that season—a subject discussed in great detail much later in a way that does not reveal my best qualities. In fact, this message gets the ball rolling a bit. 2002 also was the year our older daughter went off to college. I missed her and perhaps this carried over into some of my posts, including this one.

But anyone who really watched this Pitt team will understand the last part of this post.

1964   Posted on 1/20/03

Team basketball vs. individual basketball. The second half was the best all-around passing that I can ever remember seeing by a Pitt team, and it involved every player.

Boeheim's comparison of Pitt's defense with the old Georgetown teams was calculated and unfair. Pitt's defense has absolutely nothing to do with the old Georgetown defense. Pitt's defense is predicated on position, balance and help. Georgetown's defense was based on pressure, speed, shot blocking and hacking, and on intimidation of players and referees. Pitt's defense is far too sound to let Boeheim give it an unfair reputation.

All that's for another day. This is the team I've been waiting for all my life. Before the 1964 NCAA finals, a journalist asked a visiting Russian coach who would win between UCLA, with no starter over 6-5, and Duke, with its huge front line. The Russian coach said UCLA. The journalist asked him how he could pick against all that size. The Russian coach said: "Yes, but UCLA is team."

Pitt is team.

17-15

| JANUARY 25, 2003 | PITT 65 GEORGETOWN 64 |
| FEBRUARY 1, 2003 | SYRACUSE 67 PITT 65 |

After surviving a surprisingly tough home game with Georgetown, Pitt traveled to Syracuse limping a bit but with its second chance at the Number 1 ranking. After off-season surgery for his Big East Finals injury, Brandin Knight was playing on a bad knee, as he did all that season, and Julius Page had injured his ankle.

This one hurt. Pitt broke out to a big lead led by Chevy Troutman and forced Syracuse out of its traditional 2-3 zone. Syracuse got back in the game with a man-to-man defense that was surprisingly effective, probably even to Syracuse. After Syracuse hit two foul shots with three seconds left to go up by two, Brandin hit a half court shot a tenth of a second after the buzzer that would have won the game. In the ensuing confusion as the referees looked at the replay, Syracuse fans stormed the court three different times.

Injuries and a Philosophical Disagreement   Posted on 2/2/03

First, some due credit to Syracuse. Warrick and Duany, embarrassed in the first game, came to play last night. McNeil showed a lot of guts on those foul shots at the end. Their defense was good in the second half.

Enough about Syracuse. I have felt for two months that the biggest issue on this Pitt team is health. It will be painful if

Pitt loses in the NCAAs. But it will be much worse if we never get to see how good this team can be.

Philosophical disagreement with B Man. I don't like being homered but it happens and I can live with it. That's not to say that Syracuse did not deserve to win last night. But I do not and will not accept that it's OK for coaches, and teams, and schools to work the refs and the league. I am well aware that it will never stop. That does not make it OK. It's wrong. And it's even worse when it is premeditated and not in the heat of the game.

[And on and on I went, harkening back to Boeheim's comments in Pittsburgh…as I say, some people never grow up.]

17-15

FEBRUARY 4, 2003	PITT 68 PROVIDENCE 61
FEBRUARY 9, 2003	NOTRE DAME 66 PITT 64
FEBRUARY 12, 2003	PITT 82 WEST VIRGINIA 46
FEBRUARY 15, 2003	SETON HALL 73 PITT 61
FEBRUARY 18, 2003	PITT 82 @ GEORGETOWN 67

Battling lingering injuries and the grinding portion of a long college basketball season, Pitt struggled for the first half of February. They bottomed out in a desultory performance against Seton Hall, a game in which it was clear two minutes in that they were not ready to play. But Pitt pushed off the bottom of the pool at Georgetown and they did not lose again for a long, long time.

I remember the Georgetown game for two other things. One was Pitt broadcaster Dick Groat, the college basketball player of the year in 1952 (and the MVP of the National League in baseball in 1960) reminiscing about his freshman basketball coach at Duke 55 years earlier, with whom he had visited that night. Red Auerbach. The other was the gracious and heartfelt comments by Ben Howland, who takes some hits later in this book, about what a great competitor Michael Sweetney of Georgetown was and how he made a point to find him and tell him that after the game.

The Crossroads

The probing, piercing, razor-sharp analysis will have to wait. This is a night for broad, sweeping, chest-thumping pronouncements based upon what, on the surface, is the scantest of evidence:

Just one game. Against a struggling team. But if you believe, as I do, that this was the crossroads game for this team and that Brandin Knight and Pitt are finally getting healthy, you could conclude, as I do, that this team might not lose again for a long, long, long time.

17-15

| FEBRUARY 22, 2003 | PITT 86 RUTGERS 65 |
| FEBRUARY 26, 2003 | PITT 75 @ VIRGINIA TECH 62 |

I get carried away in March.

March   Posted on 3/1/03

A college basketball season builds slowly. They win. Sometimes they lose. The games start to get tougher. Problems are solved. Or they aren't. Players emerge. Others fade.

In March it gets very emotional, very quickly, and it is on us now.

In five days, Brandin Knight, Donatas Zavackas and Ontario Lett never will play another game for Pitt in Pittsburgh.

The Big East Tournament. Then the NCAA, or to use Ben Howland's fitting throwback term, the N-C-Two-A. Before Pitt showed us the drama of the Big East Tournament, before there even was a Big East Tournament, there was the N-C-Two-A. I have watched it unfold for nearly 40 years.

In the late 1970s, long before the NCAA office pools that now are ubiquitous, a friend introduced me to a "player pool" where a group of us would draft players on the tournament teams, rather than pick teams, and follow their scoring through the tournament. For 25 years, with friends from around the country, the "pool" has been the way we have celebrated the NCAA Tournament. No money. Just glory. And a trophy.

41

March From A to Z:

A. Dave Bing, Vaughn Harper and Richie Cornwall for Syracuse against Duke in 1966.

B. Listening to Kentucky (Louie Dampier, Pat Riley, Larry Conley, Tommy Kron and Thad Jaracz) all that year on a Kentucky radio station you could pick up in Pittsburgh at night, all the way to the historic national championship game against Texas Western.

C. Kentucky center Dan Issel, another radio favorite, fouling out on an away-from-the-ball charging foul against 5-10 Vaughn Wedeking and Jacksonville in the 1970 Mideast Regional Finals.

D. Austin Carr and the day he put up 61 points against Ohio U, in the first game on the first Saturday afternoon on NBC.

E. Pembrook Burrows III.

F. Bill Walton against Memphis State in 1973. 21 for 22. As otherworldly as Walton was on Monday night, Ernie D. was just as good on Saturday afternoon.

G. "The Great David Thompson" as he was always known in the kids' bedtime stories.

H. Rooting for Duke and Spanarkel, Gminski, and Banks in

1978. We ran into Gminski in a bar in Pittsburgh in the early 1980s. He was in for a wedding. Nice guy. A friend took the opportunity to introduce himself: "Hi, I'm Chip. I went to Carolina. I hated you."

I. Driving to a high elevation in 1979 to pull in the first NCAA scores from KYW in Philly and realizing that we were going to be doing this pool for a long time.

J. In school in Ann Arbor, watching Magic Johnson and Michigan State all that year on Channel 6 from Lansing on an old black and white TV. Then watching them blow away Notre Dame right after St. Patrick's Day, a game that started and pretty much ended with a tic-tac-toe play on the opening tip.

K. The greatest ten seconds in basketball history: Arkansas over Louisville on a half-court shot by U.S. Reed, cutting instantly to Rolando Blackman of Kansas State in the deep right corner taking down Number 1-seed Oregon State and Steve Johnson ("the Big Moose with the Big Caboose"), all narrated flawlessly by Bryant Gumbel from the NBC studio.

L. Watching with a bunch of law school buddies who had gone to Notre Dame as Danny Ainge of BYU went through the whole Notre Dame team.

M. For Georgetown in 1982 and never again until Big John left.

N. A friend's graceful exit from pool contention; first Saturday every year: "Shabbat Shalom."

O. Deciding, with a friend, that the day that Bobby Knight and Digger Phelps are out of the NCAA Tournament is the first day of spring.

P. Getting off a plane in 1986 to hear that Indiana and Notre Dame had lost in the first round to Cleveland State and Arkansas-Little Rock.

Q. A friend's lament on having to miss the pool: "I can't believe it. There are only like four things a year I look forward to, and two of them happen in my bedroom."

R. Curry Kirkpatrick's articles.

S. Carrying my three-year-old daughter in the ocean in Florida in 1987, both of us singing "Walk Like a Tarkanian." Then, startling my infant younger daughter after Chris Blocker's long jumper sent UTEP into overtime against Arizona in Tucson.

T. The curse of Barry Goheen.

U. A friend's job interview: "I'm a hard worker. But I'll need four days off in March, and I'm going to need them for the rest of my life."

V. Bo Kimble's left-handed foul shot for Hank Gathers in 1990, a shot that held a special meaning to my sister and me.

W. Watching that year as the first great UConn team beat Clemson at the buzzer on Scott Burrell's miracle pass and Tate George's miracle shot. Not being able to move a muscle because my infant son was asleep on my lap.

X. Buying a Stanley Cup style trophy for our pool and including first, second and third places because I had won twice but finished third eight times. To which another friend, then a six-time winner, replied: "I agree. It's important. I wonder who finished third in World War II?"

Y. Coppin State.

Z. Vowing that I never would have a partner in the pool, taking on the only one I ever could—my son—and together, winning for my third time ever, 1982, 1992 and 2002, or as my friend says: "Almost as often as by random chance."

It's March. It's time.

17-15

MARCH 2, 2003 | PITT 71 UCONN 67

Pitt-UConn. Again.

U-C-O-N-N UCONN!! UCONN!! UCONN!!   Posted on 3/3/03

UConn is my favorite team for Pitt to play, as long as they
don't do it very often. The three most intense games I've seen
Pitt play in the past five years were against UConn: the
crushing loss in 1999 that launched UConn on a path to the
national championship, the Big East Finals last year and
yesterday. It seems like the same game to me, and it is
exhausting just to watch.

There have been other good teams lately in the Big East. But
nobody brings it in the Big East these days like UConn. Unless
it's Pitt.

Yesterday was a test of talent and a test of wills. UConn may
not have played their best, but I'm pretty sure they played
their hardest. It seems like they never quit, at least when they
play Pitt. At the point in the game when most teams give up
and mail it in, UConn didn't. Instead they came roaring back
and almost stole it like they did in 1999. They reflect the
fighting spirit of their coach, and I mean that in the best sense.

17-15

MARCH 5, 2003	PITT 86 SETON HALL 54
MARCH 9, 2003	PITT 56 @ VILLANOVA 54
MARCH 13, 2003	PITT 67 PROVIDENCE 59
	[BIG EAST TOURNAMENT]

After blowing out Seton Hall on an emotional Senior Night for Brandin, Donatas and Ontario, Pitt almost lost a ten-point lead in the last minute against a Villanova team depleted by "phone card" suspensions. Pitt had not lost since the "crossroads" game at Georgetown and went into the Big East Tournament as regular season champion at 13-3 and the Number 1 seed.

The Providence game was stressful, though, and much closer than the final score, largely thanks to the superb Ryan Gomes and excellent play by freshman point guard Donnie McGrath. Chevy Troutman was hurt but Donatas Zavackas hit several crucial shots, after each of which my son and I jumped up, made the sign for a three-pointer, and, in our best Lithuanian accents, shouted the first two words we ever heard Zavackas say, the second of which was "you."

The First Day of Basketball Season   Posted on 3/13/03

Neutral court, single elimination college basketball. Joy of my life. Once again, I am laughed out of the family room when I suggest, as I do every year, that it is all a metaphor for death.

It's been a heck of a day of basketball. Let's start with the Pitt game, of course:

My satisfaction with Pitt winning a tough, gritty game is tempered by the nagging feeling that has bothered me all year: Is this team ever going to be healthy enough to show what it can do?

Pitt is like a finely-tuned watch. When all of the parts are working it is a beautiful thing. But they need every part. Time after time with Chevy out, Pitt worked the ball until it reached a player who just isn't quite as good, no matter how hard he tries, and everything just stopped.

If Chevy is reasonably OK, I pick Pitt over BC. I think UConn will beat Syracuse.

I like Pitt's chances better against Syracuse. Beating UConn would be more satisfying.

17-15

MARCH 14, 2003	PITT 61 BOSTON COLLEGE 48
	[BIG EAST TOURNAMENT]

Of course Brandin sprained his ankle, to go with Chevy's. Nevertheless, Pitt put BC away early, setting up the rematch of the epic 2002 Big East Final with UConn, who, in the second game, slaughtered soon-to-be national champion Syracuse.

Again   Posted on 3/15/03

The two elite teams in the Big East meet in the final of the Big East Tournament. A rematch of the best college basketball game of 2002.

A little while ago, Brandin said on Channel 2: "I'll be in the line-up tomorrow. I wouldn't miss it for the world."

I am rapidly coming to the view that I like Championship Week as much or more than the NCAA Tournament. Even though I loved the basketball part of going to the Big East last year and I'm sure I will go again some time, I think I'm enjoying the games all over the dial more this year.

But I will be sorry not to be there tomorrow when Pitt finally wins the Big East Tournament.

UConn is very, very good. It is tough to beat a good team twice in two weeks. UConn is much healthier than Pitt.

UConn matches up very well with Pitt on the perimeter and it has the equalizer inside in Okafor.

So why will Pitt win?

Because they will. Because I choose to believe they will. Because they have to. Because *they* think they have to.

Because they have unfinished business.

17-15

MARCH 15, 2003 | PITT 74 UCONN 56 [BIG EAST FINALS]

*"We have just been informed that Julius Page is the Big
East Championship Most Valuable Player. And again typical
of Pittsburgh, Len, it could have been Knight, it could have
been Zavackas, it could have been Brown, it could have been
Troutman, it could have been Lett."*
–Dan Shulman, ESPN.

*And when Brandin Knight exploded across the TV screen to steal
a ball that UConn had rolled in to save time, a startling play I have
never seen before or since, one that meant nothing to the outcome
except for the focus, intensity and intelligence it reflected, it
captured every emotion I felt and still feel about that team.*

Every Once in a While, Life Can Be Almost Perfect

Posted on 3/16/03

It is a privilege to watch them play basketball.

And a little bit humbling.

I don't know these kids or these coaches. I'm sure they have their
flaws and I know they will have their ups and downs in life. But
they will always know that there was at least one time in their life
when they were at their best, and not just as athletes.

I watched the game with my parents, my wife and our son. Three
generations, ages 14 to 78, but all feeling exactly the same way

about this team. My mother asked what that was when Brandin dove for that rolling ball. I told her that it was a triumph of the human spirit.

It is hard to keep that spirit together. Pitt has had it for more than two years. Winning helps. I am sure that Brandin Knight is central to what's going on out there. I'm equally sure that Pitt will play like this as long as Ben Howland is the coach. If he should ever leave, I would do what I often think is a bad idea, and hire an untested assistant, Jamie Dixon, just in the hope that Pitt would continue to play basketball like this.

I also wanted to say a word about Ricky Greer. He was a big part of building this. Chad Johnson, too. This did not happen overnight.

For months, it seemed that Pitt would never get healthy enough to show the country what kind of team they have. They showed them tonight. With nagging injuries all year, this team is 26 and 4 in one of the top conferences in the country. Pitt is not hot. Pitt is good.

Pitt would have beaten any team in the country tonight.

Calhoun was gracious and insightful after the game. I particularly liked that he said that he cared very much about this game. He did not try and pull a Lute Olson or, so I hear,

Roy Williams, and explain that conference tournament games don't matter. Or maybe Ben should call the selection committee and explain that the loss at Seton Hall really was not important for Pitt, even if you and I know it was the crossroads. Which leads, naturally, to...

Seeding. Pitt is not the fourth Number 1 seed. Pitt is the third team in this tournament behind Kentucky and Arizona, in that order. In fact, Pitt's accomplishments stack up quite nicely against Arizona's, and Pitt's playing better.

Pitt deserves the Number 1 seed in the East. Frankly, there is not a serious debate. If Pitt is a Number 2 seed in the East behind Kansas or Texas it would be wrong but I can live with that, because I think Pitt is better. But if Pitt is moved out of the East, especially if it put in the same region as Kentucky or Arizona, it will be grossly unfair.

It might end up being unfair to Kentucky or Arizona.

17-15

| MARCH 21, 2003 | PITT 87 WAGNER 61 [NCAA TOURNAMENT] |
| MARCH 23, 2003 | PITT 74 INDIANA 52 [NCAA TOURNAMENT] |

Ranked fourth in the country, Pitt was shipped out of the East to Minneapolis via Boston. As a Number 2 seed. Where Marquette and the University of Wisconsin were waiting from the state next door—not to mention Kentucky, the top-ranked team in the country. While Syracuse, the third place team in the Big East, got to play in Albany as a Number 3 seed in a weak regional after a blowout loss to the UConn team Pitt beat the next night by 18. Not that I'm bitter. But for a while it looked like it wouldn't matter.

Halfway Between Boston and Minneapolis   Posted on 3/25/03

That's where Pitt is. That's where we are.

It is such a pleasure to watch this team come to full flower. Some observations from the best weekend of the year for basketball fans, starting, of course, with your Pitt Panthers:

Pitt was 15-20 points better than the other seven teams in Boston, including Syracuse.

Pitt is at the top of their game defensively. On offense, they can play much better.

Finally, Pitt is almost healthy. Brandin is starting to cut like he can. Julius is almost jumping like he can. Chevy is almost running the court like he can.

I propose that people stop calling Jaron Brown "the glue." That is a term typically used to describe a player who does all of the little things but can't do the big things. It usually is reserved for a step slow white guy and, then, typically accompanied by implicitly racist terms such as "heady," "steady" and "gutty." I prefer Jaron's own description in last week's paper: "I feel like I'm just as good as anybody on our team."

My favorite moment in Boston: sitting with my Boston cousin, who once told me she went on a double date that included Ernie Davis when she was a student at Syracuse over 40 years ago, but who probably has been to four college sporting events in her life, three of which were Pitt games with me. "What did you think of that woman behind us giving a running commentary the whole game?" "That's OK. That was Brandin Knight's mother." Believe me; the apple did not fall far from the tree.

My second favorite moment: Brandin's crosscourt bullet pass intended for Jaron that hit Chevy square in the gut and Chevy laid it in without even blinking. (Digression: sitting courtside, we have come to learn that these guys—and not just Pitt guys— are so tough it's ridiculous. But are they tougher than hockey players? As my son and I joke: "Kasparaitis re-attaches his head and skates up ice.")

And from 11 hours in front of the TV on Saturday at my sister's house:

Arizona is whistling past the graveyard. First, they didn't care if they won their conference tournament. Now, Luke Walton says Gonzaga is as good as any team he's played in five years. Really? As good as Duke in the national championship game with Jason Williams, Shane Battier, Carlos Boozer and Mike Dunleavy? I have another theory. Arizona is not that good.

Far be it from me to question Lute Olson. He's won a national championship and I'm here posting on this message board. But as Arizona's star freshman, McDonald's All-American Hassan Adams, played 4 minutes out of 50 on Saturday, Ben Howland was taking another step in the masterful, season-long process of integrating his freshman, Carl Krauser, into the rotation.

Any one of the four teams could win that over-hyped region. I guess somebody has to win the East. The South is not a bad regional if they took it out of the state of Texas, where UConn would have every chance to win it.

So I agree with DT who agreed with me. I'm more upset—not less—about this bracket after last weekend. Marquette is a good team deserving of its seed. Maybe they will beat Pitt in front of a home crowd. I don't think so. I think Pitt and Kentucky are the two best teams in the country.

To those of you in a love-fest with Syracuse, let me suggest that you might be singing a different tune next week when a patently inferior Syracuse team gets Pitt's slot in the Final Four because they got Pitt's rightful slot in the East Region. I have no problem with Syracuse. I rooted for them up in Boston on Sunday. But it was wrong on Selection Sunday and it's still wrong.

17-15

2002-2003 RECORD: 28-5

Lots of time to heal, to reflect, to reconsider. Not yet.

A Sacred Trust   Posted on 3/31/03

I'm getting a little less resistance at home to the metaphor for death thing. It is the last moment of childhood for these players and that is not a metaphor.

Partly for that reason, I won't jump all over Donatas Zavackas, as surreal as that was. *[In the middle of the second half, Donatas took his shoes off and sat on the floor in the corner by the end line. I still wonder what he was thinking.]* Contrary to what I heard many other Pitt fans say, he has to answer to himself, his family and his team, and not to a bunch of people he does not know and who do not pay him. He's also a young man. He's going to have a hard enough time dealing with this, especially over time, and to live with that cloud over what was a good, hard-earned college career.

It probably would have happened eventually. Every team loses but one. Marquette was the better team on Thursday night and they may well have beaten Pitt on a lot of nights. Dwyane Wade is a great player. I think they will lose to Kansas, but

Marquette is a very deserving Final Four team and an inspiration to medium-budget schools everywhere.

There also was much to be proud of on Thursday night, especially the unconquerable fighting spirit of Brandin Knight and, really, everyone out there, as Pitt fought back through many different kinds of adversity at the end of that game and almost made it all the way back. One lasting image I have is of Carl Krauser, alone, exhorting the crowd to make noise on Travis Diener's two missed foul shots down three with two and a half seconds to play. If life really was perfect, Carl's indomitable will would have been rewarded and he would have made that three-quarter court shot Barry Goheen style.

This team and this season, really the last two seasons, have been a treasure. One that will last with me forever and will be an important part of the time we have spent together as a family.

But I am miserable.

Because this team, the team I have been waiting for all my life, was not together at the end. That was not Pitt basketball Thursday night, win or lose. Midway through the first half, I found myself explaining to my guests from Minneapolis who joined us at the game that the team I had been telling them about was not the team they were seeing.

Maybe it was just one of those nights, when the help defense was just a half-step late and the communication just wasn't quite right. Maybe Marquette is even better than I appreciate. But maybe it was something else.

If the news reports of his courtship of UCLA are accurate, and to my knowledge he has not denied them, I think Ben Howland breached a sacred trust with his team last week. The reason that this team was so special was that Ben Howland and his staff persuaded a bunch of young men from diverse and often difficult backgrounds, young men with whose care he had been entrusted, that the good of the group was more important than the interest of any individual. Then, at the crucial moment, Ben put his own interest ahead of his team's.

It's not the leaving. That happens. Ben Howland owed it to his team not to create a distraction at the summit of all they had worked for over many years. If he wanted to pursue this, he could have contacted UCLA and said that he would talk to them. After the season and on one condition: that he had a team to coach that demanded and deserved his full attention, and that any breach of that confidence would terminate his interest. Better still, he could have waited until after the season.

Did Ben Howland's sideshow affect the team? I'm not sure that ever can be fully known, certainly not by me. I'm not an "inside information" guy, and I don't want to be. Maybe I'm all wet. Surely, I am naïve. But I will always wonder. I will always wonder if Pitt could have been the team that cheated death and won the whole thing.

17-15

There was debate on the Board for a long time after this game, good debate, especially with the insightful B Man, over whether Marquette and Dwyane Wade were just too good for Pitt. Now that Wade has confirmed his greatness in the NBA, that likely will be the view of history. I never will be persuaded of that, especially the way that Pitt was out of synch in the extended time that Wade was out of the game. And Marquette did lose by thirty-three to Kansas in the Final Four. While this debate was going on, Ben Howland left and "we" had another decision to make.

The Case for Jamie Dixon   Posted on 4/1/03

The guy I really want would be sweet payback to UCLA. Unfortunately, he's 92 years old.

Failing that, I'm for Jamie Dixon...

17-15

As I look back on these last few messages I wish I was a better person and that I did not take all this so seriously. But I'm not, and I do, and this story would not be honest or complete without them.

The End   Posted on 4/8/03

Sadly, the 2002-2003 college basketball season is over. I hope and expect that over time, the lasting memories for me and my family will be of watching a team play the greatest game in the world the way it was meant to be played. Whatever else I feel about Ben Howland, I thank him for that. And if the goal is to leave a job better than you found it, it is hard to imagine anyone beating that standard by a larger margin than Ben Howland. Ben Howland was a truly inspired hire, one who turned around a program many thought could not be turned around, and who left Pitt with a very bright future. He also left Pitt with Jamie Dixon, who is central to that future.

It was thrilling to watch Pitt win the Big East Tournament. I disagree with the people who downplay the conference tournaments—at least that one. The Big East Tournament is a big deal to every team in the league. It always has been. I am quite sure that we still will watch the tape of that game 30 years from now. We will watch last year's Big East Final too. It's not only about winning.

It also was satisfying to confirm that Pitt was playing college basketball at the highest level this year. With the possible exception of Kansas in the national semi-finals, I did not see

WE ALL WE GOT

any team in the NCAA Tournament that could have beaten the Pitt team that beat UConn in the Big East Finals. As we suspected, the Big East was very, very good this year. In fact, if UConn had not been forced to play Texas in Texas, and Pitt had held it together, the Big East might have had three teams in the Final Four. And, with all due respect, Syracuse would have finished third again.

Credit Syracuse. They were given an opportunity that Pitt had earned and that was deeply wrong, but they ran with it. So as to not be completely ungracious, I thought the Syracuse freshmen were spectacular, especially Carmelo Anthony, who played not just with great ability but with a control and maturity that were way beyond his years. Gerry McNamara was great, too, but in the end it was Anthony who wanted the ball. He rightly will be remembered as one of the all-time great Final Four players.

Still, it's going to take time. The last two weeks have been so disheartening. I don't know what bothers me more: watching Syracuse win the tournament with Pitt's draw or watching Ben Howland undo, so quickly, so much of what he and many others had painstakingly built over the last four years that, to most people, Pitt will be remembered, if at all, as a footnote to the 2002-2003 college basketball season.

This was a great and beautiful basketball team and it deserved a lot more than that.

All of this can be hard to explain to a 14-year-old boy, especially when you take it too seriously, as we do. I told him the following right after the final game, and I paraphrase:

"If you are going to love college sports, you need to understand that it is an inherently flawed system, that it is not going to change, and that what you are seeing is not an exception or an aberration. Instead, if you love college sports you are going to see some of the best aspects of life and some of the worst and often you are going to see them at the same time. The best things almost always are going to involve the kids and the worst things almost always are going to involve the adults."

In my more honest moments, I confess that this drama, including the unfairness and the window into the dark side of human nature, is part of the attraction for me.

Finally, thanks to everyone here for all of your thoughts and for listening to mine. I have really enjoyed it. Next season is a new journey. I will not forget this one.

Regards.

17-15

CHAPTER THREE

31 AND
FREAKIN' 5

Hope springs eternal. This was a response to "Midnight Blue" the night I first saw Aaron Gray play, at an all-star game at the Pete. Aaron Gray was not heavily recruited. He barely played his first two years at Pitt. But you could see it, and my son and I both saw it that night.

Hello MNB   Posted on 4/15/03

Long time, no talk.
I think Aaron Gray will play in the NBA someday.

17-15

| NOVEMBER 14, 2003 | PITT 71 ALABAMA 62 |
| | [MADISON SQUARE GARDEN] |

There are a number of people who carry the Board all year long. I am not one of them. It takes me a while to get into it. So I get called out every once in a while, including after Pitt easily handled an Alabama team that ended up going to the Elite Eight in 2004.

Re: 17-15 where are you?   Posted on 11/24/03

I am not really locked into basketball yet, although I finally did bear to watch the tape of the Marquette game last night. Not a bad place to start in forming early thoughts on this year's team. My short answers are these:

I am not capable of describing how spectacular Brandin Knight was at the end of that game.

Sadly, Brandin is gone. Carl cannot control tempo like Brandin or defend as well as Brandin but he brings one or two things that Brandin did not. Overall, the task as I see it is to let Carl help shape the identity of this team without running amuck. I would say, so far so good, even if I suspect that some of the older players are adjusting to this too.

Regards.

17-15

DECEMBER 30, 2003 | PITT 76 GEORGIA 55

Mark McCarroll, 26 points. Everyone should have at least one game to remember, even if it was in the synagogue league in 1973.

One Step at a Time   Posted on 12/31/03

It was Mark McCarroll's night. That gorgeous UCLA bank shot? Was that David Meyers? Marques Johnson? Edgar Lacey?

My only problem with Mark shows how far he's come. Two years ago, my wife promised one of our friends' kids that she would buy him a box of popcorn if Mark ever scored 10 points in a game. For two full seasons, it was a safe bet. Now it's popcorn almost every night, a hotdog here and there, and last night a demand for a steak dinner.

An aside: McCarroll was asked on the post-game show whether Chevy was the strongest player he's played against. Without hesitation, Mark said, no, it was Ron Artest...

17-15

In the preseason, Pitt was ranked around Number 22. It was becoming clear that they were even better than that, again. Along with the proven nucleus of Jaron, Julius and Chevy, Carl was starting to take control at the point. Pitt also was getting a huge lift from 6-9 freshman center Chris Taft from Brooklyn, Pitt's most highly-recruited player in years, who was playing even better than expected. Mark McCarroll was helping too, as were three other freshmen who would become much more prominent down the road: 6-3 guard Antonio Graves from Mansfield, Ohio, and two big white kids: massive 7-0 Aaron Gray from across the state in Emmaus, Pennsylvania, who came in at 300 pounds and eventually got down to 270; and a 6-9 free spirited, cliff-diving redshirt freshman from Vancouver, Levon Kendall, named for Levon Helm of The Band.

"Pre-Season" Summary   Posted on 1/4/04

They have played 14 games. It seems like a good time to take stock. Here's one important thing:

Pitt is 14-0.

Pitt has beaten teams who have beaten other good teams. Georgia beat Georgia Tech the same week Pitt beat Georgia by 21 without Krauser. Florida State beat Maryland right after Pitt beat Florida State. Alabama beat Oregon and Wisconsin.

Here's another important thing:

Jamie Dixon looks comfortable in this job.

Pitt has five who look like they can compete with just about any five in the country. Carl has taken the reins from Brandin pretty darn well, even if there is still some work to do, and probably a couple of bumps in the road, before everyone plays beautiful music together. Julius and Carl are volatile, emotional players with strong personalities. Taft may be one too, although it is hard to tell whether it's him or his game that's so explosive.

But Jaron and Chevy are like rocks.

14-0. As Louie Carnesecca used to say: It's cold. It's dark. It's time for the Big East.

17-15

| JANUARY 6, 2004 | PITT 78 VIRGINIA TECH 59 |
| JANUARY 10, 2004 | PITT 84 @ MIAMI 80 (2OT) |

Pitt was 16-0 and Carl Krauser was continuing to settle in at point guard. He saved the Miami game with a coast-to-coast dash to send it into overtime. A couple of years ago, Perry Clark, the Miami coach that day and a pretty good coach in my book, was announcing the Pitt-Marquette game and said that he remembered Carl very well from that game. I would have sent him a dollar had he added, "In fact, he's a big reason that I'm sitting here right now."

My son, however, was struggling some with Carl's playground-hewn style and, even more, with me defending Carl. At a formative age, he had watched Brandin Knight show how the point guard position should be played and that, as I would come to learn, was that.

Morning After Thoughts   Posted on 1/11/04

We had a birthday party for my father-in-law yesterday and ended up with about 20 people ages 8 months to 86 watching the Pitt game in a pretty small room. My brother-in-law, in from Providence, and his family. My wife's cousin we sit with at the games and his wife, who I insist must sit to my right. Our good friend, who compares every Pitt athlete to "the Dorsett standard." Our Cleveland cousins came in too. Quite a thrill, and again to watch it on tape last night. Watching Krauser's drive and the whole Pitt bench mobbing him, my wife and I agreed: the pure joy of youth. That's college basketball.

The Krauser debate continues a bit in our house, especially because yesterday's mutual high pick-and-roll fest turned this into an NBA style dribble-athon, albeit a modestly fascinating one. But nobody in our house disputes that Carl is not afraid of anything or anybody.

Here's an odd comparison for Jaron Brown: Jaromir Jagr. In his prime, Jagr was the greatest third-period hockey player in the world because he just wore out teams by then with his physical play. I see a lot of that in Jaron at the end of games.

16-0. More tough games ahead, and probably some losses soon. But yesterday shows that this team will not crack at the first sign of adversity.

17-15

JANUARY 12, 2004	PITT 74 NOTRE DAME 71
JANUARY 17, 2004	PITT 59 RUTGERS 49
JANUARY 19, 2004	UCONN 68 PITT 65

As has happened a remarkable number of times in the past seven years, Pitt gained more credibility in a courageous defeat at UConn, in which Carl Krauser had 24 points and freshman Antonio Graves missed a good look at a three to tie at the buzzer, than in the 18 straight victories that preceded it.

UCONN   Posted on 1/24/04

"Pitt looked like Pitt." That was something we had suspected but could not know for sure until they played a really good team on the road.

I would add though that the "Pitt looked like Pitt" view was not unanimous in our house. So, perhaps, it should be "Pitt pretty much looked like Pitt, but without Brandin, without as much in transition, without as much depth, without getting Julius in the flow at key times, sometimes a little less help defense, and without getting as many good looks for Chevy, but with more points from Carl, blocks from Taft and with Jaron in the post at 6-2 and a half." Or something.

I really like the way UConn plays. I love the way Okafor conducts himself and I will pay Taliek Brown the high compliment that he plays like a Pitt player. If Pitt can't win the national championship this year, which would require a lot of moons aligning, I would be very happy if UConn, which can, did.

17-15

Led by star freshman center Chris Taft, Pitt sliced up the Syracuse 2-3 zone by feeding the high post and beat Syracuse by double figures for the fourth time in five games. It was a 21-point road win over what turned out to be a Sweet 16 Syracuse team.

"We Finally Played Like Last Year"   Posted on 1/24/04

Everybody's happy.

Except I'm starting to care too much again.

76-12. It's like a dream.

17-15

JANUARY 28, 2004	PITT 68 BOSTON COLLEGE 58
FEBRUARY 4, 2004	PITT 71 ST. JOHN'S 51
FEBRUARY 7, 2004	PITT 66 @ NOTRE DAME 58
FEBRUARY 9, 2004	SETON HALL 68 PITT 67 (2OT)

After another slugfest with BC and the superb Craig Smith, an easy win against a crumbling St. John's team that was to fall off the edge that night in a strip club outside Pittsburgh, and an impressive comeback win after falling behind 15-2 at Notre Dame, Pitt lost in double overtime on the road to a good Seton Hall team with a great guard, Andre Barrett (20 points and 6 assists), who had a terrific battle with his old New York City buddy Carl Krauser (23 points, 3 assists).

The Hall and Everything After   Posted on 2/14/04

Anymore, and I am the worst offender, we are so caught up in what a game will mean to seedings, rankings, the RPI and my new favorite, the Pomeroy Index, that we do not always stop and just enjoy the game.

That was a great college basketball game the other night between two fine teams, with streetwise and talented point guards who know each other and who went at each other for 50 minutes, and with the kind of momentum swings that are the hallmark of any great basketball game. Sure, Pitt had plenty of chances to win, but once Seton Hall got a breath of air from Pitt's suffocating defense with the three-pointer that closed the gap to 55-52, it was clear that either team could win that game. Two father-son moments:

1) Just before it happened, when Pitt was up 56-54, I said to my son: "Do you have any doubt that the Hall is coming down and hitting a 3?" Him: "None."

2) Three minutes after the game, at, literally, the same instant: "Even game."

So Seton Hall is in the books and it's time for UConn. UConn can win the national championship. UConn is capable of running almost every team in the country off the floor. I won't say they can run Pitt off the floor until they do it. If Pitt can control tempo, which I think they can, and keep Jaron, for whom UConn has no match-up, out of foul trouble, I think Pitt will win. Let's call it 67-62. Pitt.

17-15

Sometimes it is good to step back and just think of the good times. Like beating that season's national champion, for the second year in a row.

UCONN   Posted on 2/16/04

I have a few thoughts to add on the game and the mystery of UConn but first I want to pay tribute to the veterans on Pitt's bench, all of whom made big contributions yesterday: Mark McCarroll, Yuri Demetris and Torrie Morris. One of the best parts of college basketball is watching players come in as kids and leave as young men, watching kids who are not players become players.

The bench was the big story yesterday, but not the only story. Jaron Brown dominated the second half of that game. I thought that it would be many years until I would be as sad about a player leaving as I was about Brandin. Jaron will be very close.

I say this as someone who believes in his game, his spirit, and what he means to this team, and as someone who has defended him for three months, but Carl's decision-making can make you want to tear your hair out sometimes.

But you can tell how much Calhoun would like to have a kid

like Carl on his team.

U-C-O-N-N.

I still would not be shocked if UConn won the NCAA tournament. Okafor is overwhelming on defense. Gordon can get his shot anytime he wants. But you do not have to be a genius to see that something is wrong with that team. Heaven knows they have not peaked too early.

Enough about UConn. Pitt is 23 and 2. All things are possible, especially when ten players contribute, including three reserves who are still plugging away after four years.

17-15

My understanding is that the title of the post below is based on something from Cervantes, who, 400 years ago, wrote Don Quixote. *I cannot confirm this myself. Although I could name the Providence starting five from 1973, Cervantes is just one of countless important people in history about whom I know almost nothing. I heard this said on a show about a coach who won about as many games as any coach in Indiana high school basketball history but never won the state championship.*

"It's the Journey Not the Destination"   Posted on 2/22/04

Although I often agree with him, Bob Smizik in his column today managed to capture exactly the opposite of my feelings for this Pitt team.

According to Bob, anything short of the Final Four will be a disappointment for this team. The rest of the season? Trivial. The Big East tournament? A money-maker. Only the NCAA Tournament will define this team and define it completely.

According to me, no matter what happens the rest of the year, it already has been another thrilling journey, for the third incredible year in a row, and nothing that happens in the NCAA Tournament will change that.

This team already has averaged 27 wins for the past three years, including lots of big ones. Those games may not matter to Bob Smizik but they matter to the team and, whether it's healthy or not, they matter to me. Not to mention just how this team plays the game, win or lose, which matters most of all.

I also disagree completely about the Big East Tournament. Great as it is, the NCAA is played every other day spread out over three weekends. The Big East is a TOURNAMENT, every night for 4 nights, with teams that know each other. If I were king, the NCAA would play the Sweet 16 to the championship on four straight nights.

I am 46 years old. I get up every morning like a kid, excited for the next game and eager to read and watch everything I can about this team. I am enjoying it with my family, and my friends, including dozens of new Pitt fans who have come along in the past few years. One of them observed that part of my personality, a central part, is that it is important to me that people enjoy what I enjoy. I'm not sure that's healthy either, but it's true.

And I will continue to enjoy, no, to treasure, the journey, wherever it leads.

17-15

After listening to Pitt struggle on the radio on the way home from the airport, I got home in time to see Pitt come back at Georgetown, led by 26 points and 9 rebounds from Carl Krauser. The other notable aspect of this game was that Julius Page, increasingly unable to lift off his bad ankle, shot 0-7, in the beginning stages of a shooting slump that would not end.

Radio Days   Posted on 2/29/04

Anymore, outside of work, there almost always is a TV on wherever I am. It's stifling sometimes. I think that Marshall McLuhan or Aldous Huxley or George Orwell or somebody had it right, although even as I write this I feel like Woody Allen should pull Marshall McLuhan out from behind the curtain like he did in *Annie Hall* to say "you know nothing of my work." Which is true, of course. Because I'm too busy watching TV.

Still, from earliest childhood, long before cable, when it was a thrill to see a game on television, radio always has been a big part of my love of basketball. I remember listening in 1963, when I was six years old, to a Pitt team with Brian Generalovich, Calvin Sheffield and Tim Grgurich while shooting a basketball into a neighbor's laundry tub. A year or two later, and for many years, I shifted my main allegiance to

Duquesne, with Frank Miniotas and Rich Carlberg and Phil Washington and Ron Guziak. I listened to the Steel Bowl in 1964 when Rick Barry scored 75 points in two games.

Except for Barry, I never saw any of those guys play. But I can picture every one of them in my mind's eye.

When I was eight, I loved listening to high school basketball on the radio. My favorite announcer was Sam Vidnovic of McKeesport, especially when he was announcing the games of his son, Glenn Vidnovic, whom I then followed on the radio through a very good career on an excellent Iowa team that also had Chad Calabria from Aliquippa (Dante's father) and two key players from an NBA Championship team in Seattle, John Johnson and Downtown Freddie Brown. I never saw Vidnovic play either. But I know his game. 6-5. Skinny, with a lot of skills, and willing to mix it up inside.

Fast forward, past listening to Kentucky and Cawood Ledford and Rupp's Runts and Mike Casey and Dan Issel. Saturday nights picking up LSU games in Pittsburgh from Baton Rouge with Pistol Pete and Al "Apple" Sanders. Sitting outside on a street and listening to Bernie O'Keefe take down Providence and Marvin Barnes just before Duquesne slipped into the abyss.

Past a Friday night with a girl who put up with driving all over town to pick up a Philly radio station to get the NCAA scores, and, after all that, pulling it in a hundred yards away from where we started, not knowing that, years later, I would build a house another hundred yards away and move in with three kids and the same girl.

A walk on a cold night on December 19, 2001, listening to a Pitt team hang tough on the road at Ohio State, and knowing what until then we only had suspected.

Almost eerily, having heard rather than seen almost every one of Pitt's few poor efforts the past three years—at Notre Dame in 2002, the first ten minutes of the Georgia game and at Seton Hall last year, and the first half against Georgetown the other night. I don't know why, on the radio, you can tell almost instantly when a team is not ready to play.

On a drive from work the other night, I listened to a long, quiet radio interview, the kind you almost never get on television, conducted by Tim Benz with Brandin Knight. I can't do it justice. Call him. Ask him to play it again. It will tell you everything you need to know about why Pitt has done what it's done the past three years.

17-15

| FEBRUARY 29, 2004 | SYRACUSE 49 PITT 46 (OT) |
| MARCH 2, 2004 | PITT 88 @ PROVIDENCE 61 |

After a wrenching overtime loss to Syracuse, Pitt rose up and pounded the 12th-ranked Friars in Providence. The Look, as it turned out, was an illusion. But Providence did not win another game the rest of the season and I maintain that, to this day, it has never recovered from that game.

The Look   Posted on 3/6/04

For better and for worse, my life is in its own rhythm these days. A wave of work and not enough sleep interrupted by the occasional respite and the odd phone call, such as one today saying that that he's been watching and the only things Pitt needs are:

  1. More good shots from Julius.
  2. More cowbell.

  Oh, and Happy Birthday.

Thanks Dad.

Still, I would not want to pass by the performance of the year not only by Pitt but very possibly by any team in college basketball. So if you are happening to read along, just pretend it's four days ago:

You pick up the paper late in the year and see scores that make you go "oh." Like Syracuse beating Pitt in overtime at Pitt. There are scores that make you go "hmm?" like Stanford almost losing at Washington State, or Duke losing at home to Georgia Tech. But it is only once in a while when you look at a score and go "uh-oh."

I guarantee that people all over the country who follow basketball, who know basketball, saw that score and went "uh oh." Late season road game. By 27 points. Coming off a loss. On one day's rest. Against a ranked team favored by two and bumped to three or three and a half by the "smart money" before the game. That had won by ten at UConn. That was playing its biggest home game in years and years and years.

You are not as good as you look on your best night. There may be a handful or two of teams that may be as good as Pitt. But Pitt is as good as any team in the country. I am certain of it.

Is it possible that with one player, Chris Taft, recruited by the "Big Schools," and him a freshman, at a school located in an area with almost no players and a modest basketball tradition, and with a coach with no real head coaching experience, this is THE team?

Not with one moon shot of a player, either, a Larry Bird or a Magic Johnson. Instead, with a whole bunch of players, every single one far better than anyone else thought. Players who fit together just right, not just this year, but for three years, so that each team could build off the accomplishments of the previous year, so that, we can dare hope that there is now a "Pitt" way to play basketball that will last beyond any player or group of players as it has now lasted beyond Ricky and Ontario and Donatas and even, remarkably, Brandin.

When you are The Team, you have The Look. The Look can be a mirage. Or it can be fleeting. Or someone can get hurt. Or something can happen. Pitt had The Look last year against UConn and Indiana.

It's possible that Providence just got rattled. My son, my caution flag, the one who is just not quite there yet with this team, saw a lot of that on Tuesday. He makes a good point; he always does. But, to me, and even if it's because I wanted to see it, Pitt had The Look .

So, as you say goodbye to Julius, Torrie and Jaron, and heaven forbid, Chris, Chevy or Carl, watch for The Look.

I think it's there.

17-15

MARCH 6, 2004	PITT 59 VILLANOVA 45
MARCH 11, 2004	PITT 74 VIRGINIA TECH 61
	[BIG EAST TOURNAMENT]
MARCH 12, 2004	PITT 62 BOSTON COLLEGE 53
	[BIG EAST TOURNAMENT]

Pitt went into the Big East Tournament with its third straight 13-3 record and another Big East regular season championship, just ahead of UConn. They were headed to a third straight classic championship game, the three games that as much as anything define this entire era.

Rivalry   Posted on 3/13/04

Brandin Knight. Caron Butler. Jaron Brown. Emeka Okafor. Julius Page. Ben Gordon. Chevy Troutman. Taliek Brown. Carl Krauser. Josh Boone. Chris Taft. Tony Robertson. Ontario Lett. Rashad Anderson. Donatas Zavackas. Denham Brown.

UConn 74 Pitt 65 (2OT)
Pitt 71 UConn 67
Pitt 74 UConn 56
UConn 68 Pitt 65
Pitt 75 UConn 68

I firmly believe that in 60 years, when I am long gone, our children will be telling their grandchildren about these players and these games. I have been thinking a lot lately about the

Pitt teams of 1927-31 that went 80-11. Are there people who still tell their grandchildren about them?

Tonight is Round Six and Big East Championship Game Three in this remarkable battle. We hope that it will go on and on. We know that it also may disappear into the mists of time, like the 1927-31 teams.

It's a rivalry for UConn. Just listen to Taliek Brown talk about how he hates Pitt. Or the UConn message board posters, like the one who says, and I paraphrase little if at all: "I know I should never root for BC, but I can't help it because I hate Pitt with every fiber in my being."

For Pitt it is THE Rivalry.

17-15

UConn went up 13-2. Pitt stormed back, behind Carl and a million steals by Jaron, to lead by nine at the half and 51-40 with eight and a half minutes to play on a sweet three-pointer by freshman Antonio Graves. Which turned out to be the high water mark that night. UConn came back again, with several big three-pointers by Rashad Anderson and Ben Gordon, and won it on a closely-guarded shot by Gordon. This was the night UConn became the championship team everyone had thought they would be. It may never have happened without the games they played against Pitt, especially this one.

Heartbreak   Posted on 3/14/04

Well, it's a little gray here, but the sun did come up this morning.

At halftime, after the best 15 minutes of basketball Pitt has played this year, maybe in many years, I said to my wife and our son that every other team in the league would be done, but not UConn. UConn has not been right all year until this weekend but it still beats with the championship heart of Jim Calhoun.

Two years ago, we could not watch the tape of the UConn game for months. A month or so after the game, I asked my son and he just said "too soon."

I watched this one, alone, early this morning. Very early. Some reactions:

Carl played 38, 40 and 39 minutes in three nights and to me it showed a bit in the last ten minutes last night. But I'll bet he could live to be a hundred and never feel more alive than he did in the last ten minutes of the first half.

Jaron looked a step behind a few times on defense compared to where I'd usually expect him to be, I suspect because of some combination of fatigue, injury and a tough opponent. But his anticipation of passing lanes was absolutely Bird-like.

I never thought I would see the night when Pitt would outscore UConn 20-0 off the bench and lose. Or the night when Torrie Morris took it straight at Emeka Okafor.

Life has not been fair to Julius Page this year. Seeing the guy he played great defense against all night hit the winning shot was just the latest cruel twist. The way he has stood up to all of it and kept playing hurt and playing hard and going to the interview room will serve him well the rest of his life.

Unlike last year when Donatas was an excellent post defender too, there is a huge gap between Chevy and Pitt's second-best post defender (who might be Jaron at 6-2). As a result, Jamie treats Chevy's minutes like gold and he sits for long stretches just to increase the chance that he will be around at the end.

Taliek Brown is a winning ball player. He confirmed his status as a curse on Pitt last night; Brown made some great plays in transition and, a poor foul shooter, he drilled two key foul shots. He also shot an air ball and a near air ball from within three feet in the last five minutes and those misses turned into five UConn points.

When it's all said and done, UConn won and I salute them. At a certain level the better team always wins.

****

This was a tough loss. Between Jaron's and Julius's ankles and DT says Carl's shoulder, Pitt came out of this tournament less healthy than when it came in. Also, Pitt's seeding is likely not to be as good as it would have been, although if Pitt drops below a Number 2 seed at 29-4 there should be an investigation.

If they can regroup, though, Pitt stands on the cusp of great opportunity. Pitt-UConn is now being talked about as one of the top rivalries in college basketball. As Bob Ryan just said on "The Sports Reporters": "I'd like to see these teams play a seven game series."

People are starting to recognize that there is something stirring about the way they play basketball.

17-15

MARCH 19, 2004	PITT 53 CENTRAL FLORIDA 44
	[NCAA TOURNAMENT]
MARCH 21, 2004	PITT 59 WISCONSIN 55
	[NCAA TOURNAMENT]

Pitt's seeding in the 2004 NCAA Tournament was among the worst in the history of the NCAA tournament. 29-4 with many, many quality wins and the only losses being two last-second road and neutral court losses to national champion UConn, a team Pitt also beat; an overtime loss to a Sweet 16 Syracuse team that Pitt also beat on the road by 21; and a double overtime road loss to a Seton Hall team that beat Arizona in the NCAAs. That's it. For which Pitt, at 29 and 4, was rewarded with not only the lowest Number 3 seed, but also with having to play Big Ten conference tournament champion Wisconsin in Milwaukee.

All of which made—and still makes—Pitt's win over Wisconsin in front of 18,000 gracious but rabid Wisconsin fans, and us, that much sweeter.

Here We Go   Posted on 3/23/04

There are tapes and tapes and tapes, hundreds of them. Tapes that never see the light of day. Tapes to watch the day after the game. Tapes to watch once in a blue moon. Tapes to watch over and over again:

UCLA-N.C.State [Final Four] 1974

Indiana State-Arkansas [Midwest Regional Finals] 1979
Syracuse @ Pitt 1987
Pitt @ Syracuse 1988
Pitt-UConn [Big East Tournament Finals]   2002
Pitt-UConn [Big East Tournament Finals]   2003
Pitt-UConn [Big East Tournament Finals]   2004

And if I can get a copy of Providence-Memphis State 1973, or even just the first half, I can someday die a happy man.

Now, there is one more:

Pitt @ Wisconsin [NCAA Tournament] 2004

This was a road game. Against a very good team, a Sweet 16 team, at least.

That they won on guts.

That they never should have had to play.

****

But there are things that just don't come across on the tape:

Players on both teams bouncing off the player of the game, Chevy Troutman.

Jaron's stop and explode spin move.

Chevy's three-point play hanging on the rim and falling in.

Julius, stealing like Jaron, taking off and almost losing the ball but dunking hard even with his bum ankle, for the first time in weeks.

Chris Taft just detonating out of nowhere on a slam-tip at the most critical moment.

Watching Carl Krauser, time and again, pulling the ball back and starting over while Jaron stood there as calm as a man fishing in a stream, and knowing that the crowd was not going to shake them.

The sick feeling every time the ball left Devin Harris's hand.

The unbridled joy of Antonio Graves.

****

So now we go.

Oklahoma State. This is not a Sweet 16 game. This is a Final Four game. 29-3 in the Big 12 against 31-4 in the Big East. Give me a break.

Oklahoma State can win this game. But Pitt's going to win this game.

Here We Go.

17-15

MARCH 25, 2004	OKLAHOMA STATE 63 PITT 51
	[NCAA SWEET 16]

2003-2004 RECORD: 31-5

I don't think it's humanly possible to say more about this game than I did. This is the short version. In the end, Pitt tried, desperately, to break through the Sweet 16 barrier after three straight tries, but they just couldn't.

That's It, Good Season   Posted on 4/3/04

It has become a tradition between my son and me that, after the last game of the season, no matter how painful or sudden the final loss, we turn to each other and say, quietly:

"That's it. Good season."

This is from the preposterous end to the otherwise enjoyable *Remember the Titans,* when Ed Henry, the coach of the team that has just lost the state championship to Denzel Washington's Titans on a 75-yard end around on the last play of the game turns to his assistant and says as calmly as a man watching the last sunset of summer:

"That's it. Good season."

There must be a lesson in there somewhere, and besides it always makes us laugh and feel a little better.

But for many people who are paid money to write about games that kids play for almost nothing and for more than a few people on this message board and others like it, they need that last loss, preferably as gut-wrenching as possible, so that they can pursue what appears to be their true passion in sports and life. Recrimination Season:

Carl dribbles too much.

Julius shoots too much.

Julius shoots too little.

Carl shoots too much.

Chevy and Chris feel lonely and unloved.

Jamie loves everyone too much to put his foot down.

Joanie loves Chachie.

Really, it's a miracle that they won a game.

****

My better instinct is just to let it pass. Far be it from me to let that get in the way. In any event, let me get off my chest what I think is a more balanced view of the Oklahoma State game and the season.

The Oklahoma State Game.

First, some due credit to Oklahoma State. I'm not sure that there are any truly great teams in college basketball anymore, and in my opinion Oklahoma State is not one, but it's a very good team. All in all they were an Eddie Sutton-coached team and on this night they clearly were the better team.

As for Pitt, my opinion changed a good bit after watching the tape. One impression did not change: that Pitt got tired in the last eight minutes and, as a team, hit the wall and had their great heart broken in the last three minutes, not unlike UConn when Pitt blew open a close game at the end of last year's Big East final.

The rest of my impression changed substantially. At the game, I thought that a bunch of little things on offense finally caught up with Pitt. A little too much one-on-one by Carl. Not working the ball as well. Not running efficiently. Not enough "passing up good shots for great shots." On the tape there was some of that to be sure.

But more than anything, THIS TEAM JUST COULD NOT SHOOT THE DARN BALL.

Time after time, there was good movement and good chemistry that led to a good shot and sometimes a very good shot. And a miss.

Sometimes it's good to step back and see yourself as others see you. Billy Packer's shortcomings are well-known and of long standing. It was nostalgic to see him reprise, 25 years later, his Indiana State bash of 1979, and it was only right that when this year's target, St. Joe's, proved him wrong they did it by beating his alma mater, Wake Forest. But when he is not colored by this transparent agenda, I have no doubt that Billy Packer knows college basketball inside out. In both the Syracuse and Oklahoma State games it was clear to me that he liked Pitt, a lot in fact, and marveled at them, as summed up best by the statement (I paraphrase) in the Oklahoma State game that "Pitt has done remarkably well for a team that has absolutely no perimeter game."

Anymore, just about every team has a serious flaw, even the best teams. Eventually, every team but one will lose (I think, hope and pray that UConn will be that team) and, usually, it is a team's flaws that take it down.

Pitt's flaw was that they could not shoot, and in the Oklahoma State game it knocked them out of the tournament. I always thought they were just about to snap out of it and shoot like they did for the first three quarters of the year. But it never happened.

The Look.

I was wrong even if, with eight minutes to go in the Big East Finals, most of America would have agreed. I thought the 27-

point road win at Providence on one day's rest after the Syracuse loss was so extraordinary and I still do. But in the happy glow of 88 points and great passing and running and dominating inside play, I overlooked the 2-9 three-point shooting against Providence. What I thought was the ebb and flow of an average shooting team was in fact the early stage of a fatal disease.

The Season.

Still and all. 31 and *freakin'* 5. I confess to having had two personal aspirations for Pitt which have had an irrational importance to me. One is for Pitt to be ranked Number 1 at a meaningful point in the season. They missed that by less than one second last year, and it might never happen. The other was 30 wins. Done.

This era, however long it lasts, will only get sweeter with age. I will remember this as a family time, of our time with our children. I doubt we ever have had a better family trip than the one we took to Wisconsin, unless it was to Boston last year visiting my sister and her family, all properly raised as Pitt fans in BC country.

So, for now, it is done. Maybe this will be it.

But it doesn't have to be.

There always is so much more to accomplish.

Team Basketball. Defense. Old School.

Let's Go Pitt.

17-15

CHAPTER FOUR
ADVERSITY

The 2004-2005 season was "just OK," even if it would have been the best year in a decade a couple years earlier. Chevy Troutman, Carl Krauser and Chris Taft were a strong nucleus, but Julius Page and Jaron Brown were gone and they never really were replaced that year. Pitt relied heavily on several young guards: freshmen Ronald Ramon and Keith Benjamin from New York, sophomore Antonio Graves, and a junior college transfer, John DeGroat, who was only 19 and was struggling to make the switch from post to wing player. It was a season that had its moments—a lot of them actually—but it was a bumpy ride and it did not end well. Trailing Carnegie-Mellon in the first exhibition game with 12 minutes to play was a pretty good clue.

The Journey Begins, Again   Posted on 11/7/04

What happens in March will have nothing to do with Pitt's neighborly gesture to Carnegie-Mellon last night. Except that it will.

First a word for the Tartans. They were great. Hopefully they will be able to tell their grandchildren that they hung with a very good team for over 30 minutes. It did occur to me that, in the grand scheme of things, the question of who were the overwhelming favorites and who were the overachieving underdogs might be a lot blurrier than meets the eye.

On to the Panthers. Basketball begins with a point guard and a post player. Few teams can match Krauser and Taft. Plus Chevy, whose game seems to be expanding. In fact, Chevy is expanding. He seems to have added 10-15 pounds of good weight.

That's the start of a great college team. As for the rest of it, the theme that comes through to me is a Race Against the Clock. Mark and Yuri have stuck it out for five years, and they can contribute to a top team. The question is whether some combination of Graves, Gray, Ramon, DeGroat and maybe Kendall can come far enough, fast enough.

With what is here and what is coming, you can see not just a team but a program being built. But this program has not had true adversity in three years. They have not had a three-game losing streak. They have not gone 20-10. Nobody, and certainly not Pitt, wins 29 games every year. To build a program, they will have to handle that some year.

This strikes me as a less predictable journey.

17-15

DECEMBER 7, 2004	PITT 70 MEMPHIS 51
	[MADISON SQUARE GARDEN]
DECEMBER 29, 2004	PITT 72 SOUTH CAROLINA 68

They had their moments, though. In Madison Square Garden against a Memphis team that was a year away from the Elite Eight, Pitt led by 18 at the half and coasted home. Over the holidays, they beat a pretty good South Carolina team. After the game, South Carolina coach Dave Odom explained that his team had been "big boyed." By Chevy Troutman, who had 20 points and 12 rebounds, and Chris Taft, the subject of the following, who is remembered far more negatively in this town than I think fair.

Taft & C.   Posted on 1/1/05

A little perspective on Chris Taft is in order. Even though he was Pitt's highest-rated recruit in many years, he was not recruited as a "lottery pick." He was ranked more like 25-50. When Taft played much better than that, he saved the season last year, and enabled a team with two gaping holes inside, replacing Lett and Zavackas, to go 31-5, make the Sweet 16 and finish in the Top 10.

As well as Taft played, though, it was clear that he had a lot of work to do, especially at the defensive end. He only blocked three shots in the last nine games. At times he was a defensive liability, including when he had to be pulled against Wisconsin because he could not guard Zach Morley, who was not even a starter.

Then comes the summer and somewhat inexplicably we suddenly hear that Taft is projected as the second or fourth pick in the NBA draft. So now, instead of a promising young player, opposing coaches start puffing him up and comparing Taft to the young Tim Duncan. I saw Tim Duncan play in person as a sophomore. Please.

Strip away the expectations, and Taft is doing pretty well. Most college teams would kill for a guy who has even one legitimate move, gets put-backs and power dunks, can run the court and can pass. He is a MAN on both boards. His defense still needs work, but he's trying. I have just one nagging issue. Pitt recruited Taft and Gray the same year. They must have assumed that they did not play exactly the same position. Until Taft can guard a power forward, they do.

Other South Carolina notes:

…I received kudos from my daughter on my bounce passes that kept the game moving after balls rolled to me courtside. As I explained, it's all about the fundamentals.

17-15

As it turned out, Bucknell beat Kansas in the NCAAs that season. Then, the next year, it beat Syracuse in the regular season and, in the NCAAs once again, beat Arkansas. So it really wasn't that bad a loss and it started a wonderful run for Bucknell. But, at the time…

Adversity   Posted on 1/4/05

Bucknell 69 Pitt 66.

The person whose basketball opinion matters most to me offered this:

"Low basketball IQ." "Poor spacing." "Move!" "They needed this."

And I swear when Pitt went into the zone I saw someone unfurl a big white flag.

But I'm OK with it. For this program to grow, it has to overcome adversity. Not an injury, not a tough loss to a good team, or even a couple of them in a row. The kind of adversity where teams that are not together fall apart. The kind we have seen here so often over the past 30 years. The kind of which they barely have had any over the past four years.

You see what you want to see. You look past things that would be obvious to a person who did not watch most of the same players win 31 games last year, or that was even better the year before and maybe the year before that. This team has talent. It has a point guard and an inside game, the *sine qua non* of a basketball team. It shoots maybe a little better. But there are problems, problems that have been pointed out in detail, by Jamie on down to this Board.

I hold any team I care about to the same standard. I just want them to be the best team they can be, whatever that is. Any team can meet that standard. Ralph Willard's first team met that standard at 10-18. Lots of teams with winning records don't.

For this team, I have an extra standard.

They need to start playing Pitt basketball.

I think they will be OK. Either way, I bought my ticket for the whole ride, including every bump along the way.

17-15

| JANUARY 5, 2005 | GEORGETOWN 67 @ PITT 64 |
| JANUARY 8, 2005 | PITT 66 @ RUTGERS 63 (OT) |

Turns out Georgetown was pretty decent too, led by freshman forward and future Big East Player of the Year Jeff Green. But that was two straight losses at home after Pitt had lost one game in the first two years the Pete was open. Pitt managed to stop the slide and tough out an overtime win at Rutgers, led by 21 points by sweet-shooting freshman guard Ronald Ramon.

Fighting It   Posted on 1/9/05

Sometimes it comes easy and sometimes you have to fight it. Yesterday was the second kind.

Pitt could have put that game away early. They could have been up 10 or 15 at the half. Every time it looked like they were about to blow it open, Rutgers would hit a bad shot. Or Pitt would foul someone with three seconds to go on the shot clock. Once they didn't put it away it was clear it was going down to the wire. And then Carl went awry. They fought Rutgers. They fought themselves.

They fought through it.

A great sage of poetry and basketball, Charlie Spoonhouer, said that there are only two great plays: *South Pacific* and put the ball in the basket. Ronald Ramon has a ways to go. But his game grows on you. After yesterday, I would add that he's tough and, behind that baby face, he's NYC all the way.

Still, he has plenty to work on. One thing is ball-handling. Which is a good segue to:

Since they are riding on his shoulders everyone should get off Carl Krauser's back.

If Carl got hurt tomorrow, it would be very exciting to watch our Panthers try to get the ball over half court the rest of the year. Carl had a nightmare game yesterday or, more precisely, a nightmare second half. I am acutely aware of The Reasons That Carl Is Not Brandin. I also am aware of what Carl does for this team. Which is everything.

Don't get me wrong. They were not a great team yesterday. They are not a great team at all. The important thing is to get better. Yesterday they got better.

17-15

JANUARY 15, 2005	PITT 67 SETON HALL 63
JANUARY 18, 2005	ST. JOHN'S 65 PITT 62
JANUARY 22, 2005	PITT 76 @ UCONN 66

After struggling to beat an ordinary Seton Hall team at home and suffering a bad loss at depleted St. John's, Pitt fell behind by 17 points at UConn on national TV and was still down 11 at the half. It was the first-ever ESPN Gameday basketball game and Dick Vitale was yammering on as always. Many years ago, Vitale was as nice as could be to our eight-year-old daughter in an isolated corner of the Charlotte airport at 11 p.m. with nobody watching but us. I need to remind myself of that from time to time.

March 6, 1988/January 22, 2005   Posted on 1/23/05

March 6, 1988.

Pitt played at Syracuse for their first Big East regular season championship.

There were players that day who probably made a couple hundred million dollars playing basketball. Derrick Coleman. Rony Seikaly. Charles Smith. Sherman Douglas.

But there was only one man.

Jerome Lane. 29 points, 15 rebounds.

Pitt 85 Syracuse 84.

WE ALL WE GOT

January 22, 2005.

Pitt played at UConn to protect their share of a rivalry that they fought for years to create and for their confidence, their self respect and their season, all of which were on the line at halftime.

There were players tonight who may earn a couple hundred million dollars playing basketball. Josh Boone. Chris Taft. Charlie Villanueva. Rudy Gay. Aaron Gray.

But there was only one man.

Chevy Troutman. 29 points. 12 rebounds.

Pitt 76 UConn 66.

17-15

JANUARY 29, 2005	PITT 76 SYRACUSE 69
JANUARY 31, 2005	PITT 86 PROVIDENCE 66
FEBRUARY 5, 2005	WVU 83 PITT 78 (OT)

With impressive wins over Syracuse with Hakim Warrick and Gerry McNamara and Providence with Ryan Gomes, it looked like Pitt was back on track. So much so that we sloughed off an overtime loss at WVU as just one of those things, when in fact it was the crossroads game for both teams, especially West Virginia, which was launched on a magical Pittsnogle journey that ended one possession short of the Final Four.

We missed the Providence game for my father's 80th birthday for which, with my wife's inspiration, we gave him a Number 80 basketball jersey in Pitt blue and gold. He proudly wore this at a sports bar in Florida while his friends toasted him. However, during the toasts, the Pitt game started on the big screen TV and one of his friends turned to my wife and said: "Look at your father-in-law. He's not even listening. He's watching the game."

L'dor, v'dor. From generation to generation.

Catching Up
Posted on 2/6/05

After a brief vacation, here are minimally varnished thoughts on the state of Pitt basketball.

As we were stuck in the Charlotte airport for nearly a day, I observed to our son that this had been a Long Day's Journey into Night. Remarkably, he reached into his backpack and produced the Eugene O'Neill play, which he was reading for school and which I then read. The following therefore will be interspersed with haunted remembrances of misspent basketball past.

Overall, Pitt is coming along pretty well, although they have a screaming need for a quality basketball player between 6-2 and 6-7. One of the reasons Pitt seems to be coming along is the emergence from nowhere of Keith Benjamin. He made lots of mistakes last night, the kind an inexperienced player makes. But he plays with an aggressiveness and physicality that add to the presence of this team. In fact:

(Haunted Digression #1: I was watching one of my five favorite all-time players the other night on Classic Sports. By his full name, and as he was referred to by the broadcast team of Jim Thacker and Billy Packer: The Great David Thompson, in the classic 1974 ACC Final against a great Maryland team. One thing Thompson did was to get up so high and so fast and kind of pull back on his jumper so that for an instant it seemed like he was floating in the air all by himself. Keith Benjamin is no David Thompson and he never will be. But his mid-range jumper is like that.)

(Haunted Digression #2: Listening to Thacker and the young Packer, it reminded me of one of the million things I liked better about college basketball as a kid, which is that the announcers did not scream and yell and act like they were the story. They just announced the game. Like Len Elmore—who played in that 1974 game, and very well—and Dan Shulman still do.)

Seeing David Thompson reminded me of something else. In my mind's eye, he was perfect. Watching him play, as great as he was, he missed shots, he turned the ball over. He made mental mistakes.

Another player who never will be David Thompson: Carl Krauser. He made mistakes last night. By his own account, he took too much into his own hands in overtime. He needs to trust his teammates more. But Krauser has been playing great basketball and he had 15 assists last night.

Krauser is not perfect. Taft is not perfect. Chevy is not perfect. Nobody's perfect.

(Haunted Digression #3: Oscar Robertson may have been perfect. I saw him on "SportsCentury" the other day and on TV many times as a kid. He was a work of art. Pure. Strong. Balanced. No wasted motion.

Michael Jordan was a great player. Maybe not as strong as Oscar Robertson but he ran and jumped better. Michael

Jordan also was not fully appreciated as one of the best defenders ever to play basketball. He played the game as it was played in his time, even if the game was shifted some to market his talents. He won, insatiably. But take away all the traveling and palming and holding and pushing and shoving in today's game and I think that Oscar Robertson may have been the best all-around basketball player.)

Oscar Robertson. Michael Jordan. David Thompson. All between 6-2 and 6-7. Just what this Pitt team could use.

I think they will be OK. Maybe not a team that fulfills all of our hopes and dreams. But one that can keep us "drunk on basketball" through another long, cold winter. That's enough for me.

17-15

FEBRUARY 8, 2005	PITT 55 ST. JOHN'S 44
FEBRUARY 12, 2005	PITT 68 NOTRE DAME 66
FEBRUARY 14, 2005	PITT 68 @ SYRACUSE 64

Although Pitt rebounded to defeat St. John's and Notre Dame, it still did not feel right. But I would be remiss if I failed to point out that Carl had a couple of teeth knocked out in the middle of the second half of the Notre Dame game and came back a few minutes later to dive head first into a pile to get a crucial loose ball. Then he drove through traffic for the winning lay-up. In so many ways, there is nobody quite like Carl.

Two days later, down eight points at Syracuse with less than seven minutes to play, Pitt rode three long bombs by Carl and double doubles by Chevy (20 and 10) and a resurgent Chris Taft to a satisfying win in the Dome, Pitt's third win there in four years. For a season that will be remembered as a bit of a downer, boy did this team have some sweet road wins.

Comeback   Posted on 2/14/05

When they were down 58-50, I said that I just wanted to see some Pittsburgh poise, the kind they have had the past three years. That wasn't enough for them.

They come to win.

17-15

| FEBRUARY 20, 2005 | VILLANOVA 80 PITT 72 |
| FEBRUARY 23, 2005 | WEST VIRGINIA 70 @ PITT 66 |

After a well-played road loss to a superb Villanova team that ended up losing to eventual national champion North Carolina by 1 in the Sweet 16, Pitt led West Virginia at home by 12 with seven and a half minutes to play, when the game, and, really, the season took a sharp left. West Virginia's 6-11 three point bomber Kevin Pittsnogle scored 20 of his 22 points in the last ten minutes. Chris Taft was playing hard and well, dominating the boards, and seemed close to finally hitting his stride after a tough season. But he sat a lot at the end. Looking back, West Virginia was extraordinarily good at spreading the court and, in fairness, maybe there just was nobody for Taft to guard. That was not how I saw it at the time, though.

Seabiscuit   Posted on 2/23/05

In the movie *Seabiscuit* there is a moving scene where the great horse finally finds his stride.

Tonight our thoroughbred was finally finding his stride. There was Chris Taft and there was everybody else. Everybody. When our thoroughbred starts to run.

Let. Him. Run.

17-15

Let the healing begin.

The Four Most Famous Letters in College Basketball

I root for the underdog. I don't know why. I am not an underdog myself. I live in the most prosperous country in the history of the world. I have a good job. I married up. I have great kids. If I had a therapist, you could ask him, but for now I get my therapy from people who, assuming they actually exist, have names like DT, B Man and Jeffburgh.

Pitt is the perfect team for me. The underdog with a chance. Just about anything is possible at Pitt, in football and basketball. The highest highs. The lowest lows. Anything. There is almost no other program like it. I have been rooting for Pitt so long that I don't know if it's because I am drawn to its special mix of possibilities or whether it has come to shape me instead. Either way, it is a defining part of my personality to root for the underdog and it has been for almost 40 years.

With one exception. What they used to call the four most famous letters in college basketball.

U-C-L-A.

In the late 1960s and early 1970s, when I was old enough to know that they were anything but the underdog, when they won 10 national championships in 12 years, when they got just about any player they wanted, I rooted for UCLA. Because what they played was not basketball, it was art. The way that they moved. The way that they were always on balance. The way that they worked together. The way that each player only did what he had shown John Wooden he could do. The way the team made the players better. The way the stars excelled without taking away from the team. They were coached by the greatest coach in any sport and they were almost perfect.

Why bring this up now? Because I watched UCLA yesterday against Notre Dame and they are starting to play that way again. Different. More physical. Less graceful. But the same.

It was beautiful to see, and very, very painful. That was *our* team out there. The way that I still hope we can be again. I think UCLA will win a national championship in the next four years. I may have to root for them to do it.

17-15

FEBRUARY 26, 2005	UCONN 73 @ PITT 64
FEBRUARY 28, 2005	PITT 72 @ BOSTON COLLEGE 50
MARCH 5, 2005	PITT 85 @ NOTRE DAME 77

The topsy-turvy season continued. After a third straight loss, at home to UConn on Senior Day—a day on which many Pitt fans did not do themselves proud—Pitt staggered off the deck and knocked Boston College, the Number 5 team in the country, straight out of Conte Forum if not the Big East. They followed this with another decisive road win at Notre Dame, led by 26 points and 11 rebounds by Chris Taft. It was a birthday weekend treat for me, especially spending it with my daughters in South Bend.

Road Trip
Posted on 3/6/05

After a comedy of errors of late starts, wrong train stations, college schedules and missed trains, we landed in our seats at the Joyce Center just as they were saying good-bye to Chris Thomas on Senior Day. And this is what we saw:

This Pitt team still has some distinct flaws. It struggles to guard the three-pointer. It is not settled at the small forward and probably won't be. It is vastly improved at the shooting guard from earlier in the year, but it is young and untested in tournament play. It is inconsistent at center, although not nearly as much as the critics have suggested. It is, no pun intended, hit or miss from the foul line.

Emotionally, I do not feel about this team like the "first team." Or the team two years ago, the purest Pitt team I ever expect to see. Or last year, when I was so relieved that it did not end when Ben and Brandin left.

But this team has now overcome adversity, adversity of the type those first three teams never faced, and it has done it twice. It may not yet have my undying love, but it has my respect. And my full attention. Just when I thought I was out, this team has pulled me back in.

Seabiscuit, Part II. Or as Lee Trevino said about Jack Nicklaus, "Let the big dog eat." When Chris Taft plays like he did yesterday, and with Chevy and Gray and Kendall, there are not five teams in the country who would not be destroyed inside by Pitt.

(Digression #1: Our travel frolics and detours led me to spend some time yesterday at the College Football Hall of Fame. I had been there once before. It was, as I had remembered it, generally disappointing. I did learn one thing this time that was startling, at least to me, courtesy of a plaque from the "End Coach" of the 1955 Northwestern team, honoring the head coach, Lou Saban. While it was interesting that Saban was the coach of Northwestern, presumably just before Ara Parseghian, more interesting, and I suspect the real reason for the plaque, was that the "End Coach," pictured in all his youthful glory, was none other than George Steinbrenner!)

"He Doesn't Know How Good He Is." Unlike his staunch supporters, and his various critics, I have been on the fence on Antonio Graves. In some ways, I still am. There are moments, like his one-on-four fast break yesterday, when I think he just does not have the basketball savvy of the "city kids." On a team that may lead the country in careless passes between the top of the key and the wings, he may lead the team.

But I am inclined to agree with what Jamie said at the beginning of the season: Antonio Graves does not know how good he is. He is the quickest kid on the team. He has excellent size. He can shoot. He can get into the lane and get his shot. As he showed on two beauties yesterday, he can use his left hand. He can pass. He can guard someone. He's a team player, and a good teammate. To me, that adds up to a potentially excellent college basketball player. And excellent is what he was in the second half of two big road wins this week.

(Digression #2: About ten minutes in, a group of people joined our little "Let's Go Pitt" section in the back of the end zone. We think it was the Graves family. They seemed very nice and I'm sure they enjoyed Antonio's fine play. The highlight, though, was looking over as they were playing the Notre Dame fight song, one of the classic songs in sports, and seeing a little girl in the group, about ten years old in pigtails, giving the Notre Dame band the two-thumbs down signal.)

I was struck by how round and intimate the Joyce Center is,

like a circus tent. It was a good crowd, although my sense is that there is more passion at Notre Dame to return to glory in football than in basketball. But there was plenty of glory there, on the 100th anniversary of Notre Dame basketball, starting with the introduction of Ray Meyer (yes, that Ray Meyer) from Notre Dame's 1936 national championship team (1936!). Then at halftime they announced the top 25 Notre Dame players of those 100 years. Many of the names brought back fond memories from my youth. The matched pair of Bob Whitmore and Bob Arnzen, and Collis Jones, and Adrian Dantley.

But, on a day that will provide many memories, there was only one moment that gave me chills: when the largest cheer, by far, was for a true childhood hero, on the same court where he put in 46 to take down UCLA—a game broadcast by TVS that I could only pull in with an almost impossibly fuzzy picture on Channel 7 in Weirton, during which, as a guy behind us reminded us yesterday, Sidney Wicks supposedly threw up his arms to John Wooden and said "I can't guard him."

Austin Carr. 34 years later.

College basketball. It's a beautiful thing. And it's March.

I'm in.

17-15

MARCH 10, 2005	VILLANOVA 67 PITT 58
	[BIG EAST TOURNAMENT]
MARCH 17, 2005	PACIFIC 79 PITT 71
	[NCAA TOURNAMENT]

2004-2005 RECORD: 20-9

It turned out that the nice wins at BC and Notre Dame were the end of the line for Pitt after all. This also marked the end of a wonderful career for Chevy Troutman, who rose from sitting the bench most of his freshman year to First Team All-Big East, one of only a handful of Pitt players ever to be so honored.

But basketball season was not over. Not in a big way, at least for some very good friends. If you subscribe, as I do, to the theory of sports and life that all sports tend to devolve into raw violence, it may just be a matter of time before they say, "There's the hoop down there, you have 35 seconds, each of you do whatever you want." It is a joy to see a team that reminds you that it does not have to be that way.

This Is Why I Love College Basketball   Posted on 3/20/05

I have been thinking about our Panthers, a team that only briefly inspired in 2004-2005, and even then more by courage and perseverance in some tough road gyms than by the special quality of team basketball. For now, suffice it to say that the personalized nature of the criticism here over the past few days is disconcerting. A friend reported to me that her husband told her after the West Virginia game that "this Pitt team is dead to me." I understand, better than most I suspect, the concern that something special might be slipping away. But to be so angry at complete strangers, children and young adults, when they don't meet your emotional needs by how they play a game? All I can say is that some people need to take a step back.

Dissecting our Pitt Panthers or their fans will have to wait for another day. Because this is about how a pure basketball team can feed the soul. Like the 2001-2002 and 2002-2003 Pitt Panthers. Or, to put it another way, how about those, no, make that our, 2004-2005 West Virginia Mountaineers.

That is one great college basketball team. And last night's game with Wake Forest was one great college basketball game, easily one of the ten best I have seen in 40 years:

West Virginia 111 Wake Forest 105. Double overtime.

It reminded me of two games from long ago. The North Carolina-UNLV national semi-final of 1977, with North Carolina of all teams as the less athletic underdog, and with Mike O'Koren playing the slicing, slashing role that Mike Gansey played last night.

And also the Mt. Lebanon-Laurel Highlands game of 1967,

with Taron Downey of Wake Forest playing the part of tenth-grader Jim Hopgood, courageously forcing overtime with a long bomb, only to fall short at the end.

There was a little Princeton-Georgetown going on here too.

Watching a team pass the ball like that is its own reward, but I confess that this game carried with it a personal satisfaction that only a relatively small number of people would fully appreciate.

Every single player on West Virginia has my complete respect. Sally. Gansey. Herber. Fischer. Pittsnogle. Collins. Beilein. Young. Nichols. I thought Collins was the weak link. Not last night. And when he went out, their freshman back-up Nichols went straight at the great All-American Chris Paul.

Because a great basketball game can lift everyone in it like a magic carpet so that they can do things they never thought they could.

Wake Forest is a great team. On offense. They might have won if, at the end, they hadn't ignored the one match-up, the massive Eric Williams inside, for which West Virginia had no answer. But I would not assume that because the more athletic team lost, the more talented team lost.

There is more to talent than raw athletic ability.

Because this is basketball. The greatest game in the world.

17-15

From the day he got here, we knew that Brandin Knight was a basketball genius.

Julius Page. Whoa.

When Jaron Brown started to play, Pitt started to win.

Donatas Zavackas. Rocky V.

Ontario Lett played with a big smile on his face and it took about a
half-hour to get around him.

Chevy.

Chad Johnson. Flying Chad.

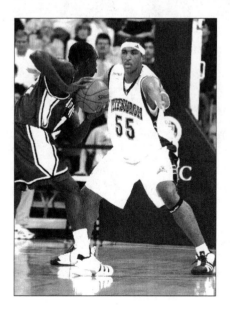

Toree Morris. A big part of a
class that won 107 games.

Mark McCarroll, childhood friend of rapper 50 Cent.

Carl Krauser, as he would let the world know, from the Bronx.

Chris Taft was Pitt's highest-rated recruit in many years. When he played even better than that, Pitt went 31 and freakin' 5.

AAAAARRWWIINNN GGGWWWAAAAYYY!!!!!!!

Levon Kendall: The Glue.

One of the great smiles:
Antonio Graves.

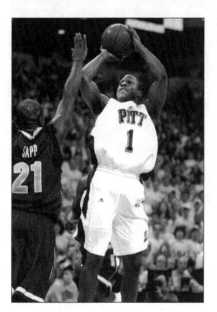

Keith Benjamin:
Senior Leader.

Sweet Ronald Ramon takes out West Virginia with the jump shot that was a small work of art.

The natural leader: Levance Fields.

Sam!!!

"They call me Mr. Biggs."

Mike Cook the basketball player was a great loss when he was injured.
Mike Cook the leader and friend remained a very big part of the team.

Gilbert the Gazelle.

There was a lot of talk about an appropriate name. Grizzly Blair. The Blair
Dunk Project. To the team, though, it was always The Big Fella.

Above and Right:
Jamie Dixon and
Ben Howland,
architects of the
Golden Era in Pitt
basketball.

A great program, probably a great anything, starts at the very top. Chancellor Mark Nordenberg, whom Coach Jamie Dixon presented with the game ball from the 2008 Big East Championship game, greets Pitt students in the Oakland Zoo.

The Pete.

CHAPTER FIVE
CARL AND THE
BIG WHITE BOYS

The great circle of life continues. Chevy Troutman graduated, Chris Taft went pro and when Carl Krauser flirted with the draft it looked like all three proven players would be gone. But Carl came back and the young players were a year older; they were joined by a junior college inside player, Doyle Hudson, from the Bahamas, who did not play much that year, and three exciting freshmen who did: 6-6 leaper Sam Young from Maryland, near DC, 6-8 power player Tyrell Biggs from Nanuet, New York, and a 5-10 bowling ball of a point guard, Levance Fields, from Taft's old school, Brooklyn Xaverian.

Still, with their starting power forward and center gone, Pitt was picked to fall back to the lower middle of the pack in the Big East. The party was supposed to be over. It wasn't. As my son and I had suspected from the first day we saw him as a high school senior, Pitt had an NBA center buried on their roster.

After the Auburn win, when Pitt was 5-0 and completely untested, I had the following email exchange with some friends at work. I went to that game at UConn, and I almost went for free.

****

Me: It's early, I will admit, but I thought you might like to know that the RPI, that bastion of integrity, and source for NCAA seeding, has 5-0 Pitt ranked well behind the 3-2 Auburn team it beat by almost 40 last week...

All this proves only one thing: despite the fact that they are completely unproven, have some obvious weaknesses and at times have been lackluster, Pitt got me interested the other night. We'll see what happens tonight and against the somewhat improved Evil Empire on Saturday. I am starting to think about the chances of Pitt being 18-0 again when they play UConn.

****

Friend: I was with you entirely until 18-0...If Pitt is 18-0 when it plays UConn, I will pay for you to fly to Connecticut to see the game.

Guys, please do not forward his email to anyone. I don't want to see men in white jackets appearing at his door.

Not so improved after all. Penn State has ended the series, citing the many schools in Pennsylvania that are anxious to play them. Perhaps this is why:

2001: Pitt 83 Penn St. 53
2002: Pitt 82 Penn St. 60
2003: Pitt 64 Penn St. 37
2004: Pitt 84 Penn St. 71
2005: Pitt 91 Penn St. 54

Good, Very Good or Really Good?   Posted on 12/18/05

We are at roughly the one-quarter pole of the season. It is too early to tell if Pitt is good, very good or really good.

The identity of this team is starting to form: it's Carl and (if you are allowed to say this) the big white boys. That's the nucleus. After that it's a cast of thousands, all promising, out of which, hopefully, at least one or two will have a good night every night. Carl is a given. The season will turn on whether Gray and Kendall continue to play at a high level against better competition, whether any of the cast of thousands steps forward to become a "nucleus" player and whether the chemistry holds up with ten players fighting for playing time.

I think that Pitt will win 19-23 games in the regular season.

That would be excellent, especially in an expected rebuilding year. More than anything, it would be a tribute to Carl Krauser, his mental toughness and to use the old-fashioned term, his will to win.

17-15

| DECEMBER 28, 2005 | PITT 58 @ SOUTH CAROLINA 51 |
| DECEMBER 31, 2005 | PITT 73 WISCONSIN 64 |

After a quality road win led by freshman Sam Young over a South Carolina team that beat eventual national champion Florida twice and then won the NIT for the second straight year, and a New Year's Eve rematch of the great 2004 NCAA tournament game against Wisconsin, Pitt was 11-0 and its record against the ACC, SEC, Big Ten, Big 12 and Pac 10 over the past five seasons stood at 17-2.

Eleven

Posted on 1/1/06

The proper number for these lists is Ten. But as they said in *Spinal Tap,* this one goes to Eleven:

1. Saddled with Fouls and with a Burr in that Saddle. I hate to start with this but one is the number of off-the-ball fouls the imperious one, Jim Burr, called on Wisconsin all night, and it was a double foul in his Javert-like quest to hunt down Aaron Gray. It's not that his calls are unfair. It's that he has such a way of making it all about him that he gets players out of their game. Coaches like him though, and they respect him.

2. Happy New Year From #2. The best thing about Levance Fields's articulate and poised post-game interview was when he wished Dick Groat and Bill Hillgrove an

unsolicited Happy New Year, which clearly surprised them both. It is always a pleasure to hear another "young man" who is comfortable behind the mike. Lot of game, too.

3. "Put In Jaron." As I said to my daughter after Alando Tucker's nine millionth post-up in a row. The three spot will have as much to do as anything with how far this joy ride will go this year.

4. The Four Freshmen. Actually, Pitt only has three freshmen but they were really good last night. I did not see Young coming this fast. In fact, he's not coming. He's here.

5. "They Call Me Mr. Biggs." I stole that one from my wife, who paraphrases one of our favorite movies, *In the Heat of the Night,* every time Number 5 does something good for our Panthers.

6. Badger Bo. I could think of a lot of good reasons why this series was scheduled. The reason I choose to believe is that Bo Ryan is a tough guy; he thinks that his team needs to be tough and that the best way to do that is to play tough teams. Pitt has now out-toughed a tough Wisconsin team in two games. (So the operative word here is tough.) That was a good team Pitt played last night and they both will be better for it.

7. Missed Blow-outs. One of the best things about last night is that Pitt missed a lot of chances to blow that game open. Pitt did not play over its head last night. If anything, it seemed to me that Wisconsin made more key plays than you might expect to stay in the game.

8. 2007-2008. Last night was the first night I could picture a really good team, not just a decent team, in the post-Carl era.

9. Number 9. Number 9. Number 9. For you *Woodstock* fans. A nine-point win. And what Pitt should be ranked next week, give or take.

10. A Team of Ten. I have been a skeptic about the ten-man rotation. I just think it is hard to maintain the flow. Still, it felt good last night to see that Pitt was never out of energy and, even better, never out of options. In fact, I would not have minded seeing Doyle Hudson last night, which might have made for point 11. Except that point Number 11 is reserved for jersey Number 11.

11. The Whole Package. I have long since come to accept that you must take the whole package with Carl. The same package that includes the passion, the leadership and the fearlessness also includes the recklessness, the sloppiness, the mouth, and the things that, to put it mildly, keep him from getting star treatment from referees. But step back and you

can see that this package includes a tremendous amount of work on his game and on his body. Watch a tape of the pudgy freshman Carl and you will be amazed at what you see now. While he always was talented, his game is so much more complete. Last night, as we were watching a great college player, Tucker, who could kill you in one way, here is what Wisconsin was seeing. A great college player who could beat you driving and finishing, driving and passing, with a pull-up jumper, with a runner, with three-pointers, defending the point guard, and the two guard and even Tucker, on the defensive boards and on the offensive boards. Who just keeps coming and coming at you.

And here is the thing. I need to whisper this out of respect to Jaron, Julius and Chevy. You are watching the third year of the Carl Krauser Era in Pitt basketball. Not as pristine and pure as the Brandin Era. A little on the "And 1" side. But very special in its own way. 31-5 special. 62-14 special. 11-0 special by a team that was supposed to slide back to the lower middle of the pack in the Big East. And who knows what else.

17-15

JANUARY 4, 2006	PITT 100 NOTRE DAME 97 (2OT)
JANUARY 12, 2006	PITT 73 DEPAUL 65
JANUARY 15, 2006	PITT 61 @ LOUISVILLE 57

Pitt rolled through the first half of January still undefeated, with a home win over Notre Dame led by 25 points and 11 rebounds from emerging star Aaron Gray, a game which Pitt won on a come-from-behind three-pointer by Ronald Ramon in the final seconds of the second overtime, surviving an amazing 37-point performance by Chris Quinn, who rallied Notre Dame from a nine-point deficit in the last 45 seconds of regulation and again from seven points down with a minute to play in overtime. Pitt handled DePaul at home behind another imposing performance by Gray (20 points, 12 rebounds), and then held off Louisville in Freedom Hall with a big contribution by the chubby freshman point guard, Levance Fields, who just got better and better all year as he became the anointed heir to Carl Krauser. During a break in the action, we went to see Glory Road, *the story of the 1966 Texas Western team, the first team to win a national championship starting five black players.*

Glory Road   Posted on 1/15/06

As we enter the heart of another season, seeing *Glory Road* reminded me of how much I love college basketball. It was a little too ABC family movie for my taste, especially in the Grated version of Adolph Rupp. There were a few small inaccuracies. JoJo White stepped out of bounds on the left wing, not the right. There was no such thing as Division I in 1966. It was not Don Haskins's first season; in 1964, he coached Texas Western with James Barnes, the original Bad News Barnes, who preceded Marvin and my personal favorite, Bad News Barnes Hauptfuhrer, of Penn Charter and Princeton.

Still, it is such a compelling story that it can't go wrong. I remember the season. I also saw a documentary on it with great actual footage and read a book on it, *And the Walls Came Tumbling Down*, which led to an amazing surprise. I mentioned this book at dinner at a firm retreat to a middle-aged health care lawyer at our firm named Murray from New Jersey, whom I had never met. It turns out that Murray was a late bloomer who got shipped out in the mid 1960s to "find himself" and somehow showed up in the middle of nowhere at Texas Western. He ended up hanging with these guys, who also were outsiders, and he rattled off all of their names to me 35 years later.

But the best thing I have ever read or seen about this story was an article by Curry Kirkpatrick in *Sports Illustrated* called "The Night They Drove Old Dixie Down." This article got to the heart of the matter and not just about Texas Western, Kentucky, Adolph Rupp and the 1960s. Curry Kirkpatrick was by far the best college basketball writer I have ever read, and he wrote with an abiding love for college basketball that predated my own.

Curry Kirkpatrick wrote of a time when college basketball was a backwater. When, as he once wrote, you could listen to games on the radio and feel like you had struck gold. As late as 1972, I remember listening to the second game of the Final Four on the radio on a Thursday night. Only the first game was on TV here that night. A favored North Carolina team with Robert McAdoo and three starters from Western Pennsylvania— Dennis Wuycik, George Karl, and Steve Previs—was upset by Florida State. In that second game, on the radio, in a battle of All-American guards, Louisville's Jim Price outscored UCLA's Henry Bibby 30-2 and UCLA still slaughtered Louisville. As Kirkpatrick explained in a moment of genius, Louisville's great power forward, Ron "the Horse" Thomas, was forced away from the hoop by the looming presence of Bill Walton where, sadly, Thomas was "a horse with no game."

It was a simpler time, when the best player in college basketball had not been shown on ESPN in nursery school. Instead, he was sitting on the back of a garbage truck in French Lick, Indiana. I looked at my *Complete Sports Basketball* magazine for 1965-66 featuring full color photographs of the All-Americans of that season—Dave Schellhase, Cazzie Russell, John Austin, Jimmy Walker and Henry Finkel—and previews of over 200 college teams, among them Adelphi, Amherst, Baldwin-Wallace, Bates, Beloit, Bowdoin, Brandeis, Colby and so on. But not Texas Western, which would be the national champion of 1966.

Pitt did make that magazine, which predicted that "the Panthers will surpass last year's 7-16 record only because the schedule is weaker." Pitt's limited tradition is part of the reason that it is treated like an afterthought when, in fact, Pitt has now been one of the ten best basketball programs in the country for a five-year period. Last week, *Sports Illustrated*, the paper of record of my youth, reduced now to the greatest and most life-affirming sportswriter in America, Steve Rushin, surrounded by a staff full of writers influenced to one degree or another by the smug "look at me" style now in fashion, wrote a long article on the Big East which included a single sentence to the effect of, "Even unheralded Pitt is 12-0." Of course they are unheralded. Four top-ten teams in five years and *Sports Illustrated* has never written an article on Pitt—not one—unless you want to count a couple-paragraph sidebar on Carl a couple of years ago, and I don't.

As you can see, part of this really steams me. But part of me likes it. In many ways this has been our little secret. Not as secret as Texas Western was in 1966. Not as important, either. Not nearly. But our secret. Part of me would like to keep it that way.

14-0. Tough as nails. With another vestige of a bygone era, a real center.

Don't tell anyone.

17-15

JANUARY 18, 2006	PITT 76 @ RUTGERS 68
JANUARY 21, 2006	ST. JOHN'S 55 PITT 50
JANUARY 23, 2006	PITT 80 SYRACUSE 67
JANUARY 28, 2006	PITT 77 MARQUETTE 71

After another nice win at the RAC, Pitt missed a chance to be the only undefeated team in the country, losing on the road to a weak St. John's team (in a game my younger daughter and I attended with some good friends) on the same day Duke lost to Georgetown and Florida lost to Tennessee. Pitt played four games that started at noon in 2005-06. They fell way behind early in all four and lost three of them. In my mind it was no coincidence. Still, Pitt bounced back with a nice win over Syracuse on Big Monday and rallied from another slow noon start to beat a good Marquette team led by 19 points off the bench from Antonio Graves. Pitt stood at 17-1 and I stood one lethargic noon loss at St. John's from a free trip to UConn.

Here's Your Chance   Posted on 1/30/06

I would like to go off on the rankings and there are ample facts to support such a rant. My heart is not in it and there will be plenty of time for that. As good as they may be, right now there is no objective basis to rank Florida ahead of Pitt. But they are a cool team, with sons of Tito Horford, Sidney Green and Yannick Noah all playing key roles. Which reminds me that at the same time that Yannick Noah was playing tennis, I had a classmate named Noah Yanich. I digress. The point is, Pitt is doing great, and I am proud of them and happy for them. But they are not setting my soul on fire. Yet.

To paraphrase a line from *Independence Day* by a fellow Pittsburgher, Jeff Goldblum, who, as it happens, is a first cousin of another classmate:

"Here's your chance."

Because when it may be the game of the year in the Big East, when it may be consistently the best game in college basketball for a five-year period, you don't waste your time on rankings. They have played eight great games the last four years. It is 4-4. Three times, win or lose, in 2002 in the Big East Tournament, in 2004 in Hartford, and last year in Storrs, Pitt used this game to show that they belonged in the highest level of college basketball.

There are times when a team that wants to be good, that thinks it's good, that knows it's good, must stand up and be counted.

Here's your chance.

17-15

A great trip with some special friends in Connecticut. On my own nickel. Another terrific Pitt-UConn game that went down to the final seconds. Aaron Gray was magnificent, with 23 points and 12 rebounds against a front line that had three NBA first-round draft choices that spring.

The Wilderness   Posted on 2/3/06

The truth lies in the middle. A team that delivers, year after year, only to be placed back in the starting block the next season as if it had accomplished nothing. Then, deep into the season, it does something, usually, ironically, losing, that makes people sit up and say "Where did these guys come from?" Next year, it starts all over again. The other view, more charitable, is that it simply takes time. In this view, Pitt is in the wilderness. It is paying dues and gaining ground.

How close will Pitt get to the edge of the wilderness this year? That depends on UConn. Because if UConn is as great as people think, then Pitt is, at least, very, very good. But I'm not sure about UConn. Close up, in person, they clearly are the best team that Pitt has played, by far. They are very athletic, deep, long and unusual in many ways, with a sometimes superstar in Rudy Gay. But UConn faces serious questions, and they do not seem to me to be the kind of prohibitive national co-favorite that they are being built up to be. They really only have one ball handler, Marcus Williams. Boone and Armstrong are good but they are not Okafor.

Still and all, UConn is very good and UConn and its fans were up for that game, in an old-time gym setting that I loved. There are only about 15-20 teams in the country who would not have been blown out of that gym on Tuesday and it started that way. But as the game went on, and even after Carl fouled out, Pitt just settled in and played their game. They just played basketball.

Pitt basketball.

17-15

A Hanukkah gift from my thoughtful and sweet younger daughter inspired this "gem." Every once in a while, it just gets away from me.

Monarchy   Posted on 2/8/06

My younger daughter recently gave me a jar of peanut butter and the book *Duel*, which addresses the circumstances that led to the duel in which Aaron Burr, our third vice president, killed Alexander Hamilton, whose face appears on our $10 bill. This gift was inspired by Pitt basketball, about which more later. It is an interesting subject, if only as a reminder of how things have changed. It is unthinkable to imagine a duel between, say, Bill Clinton and Dick Cheney. Isn't it? In other ways, though, the world is exactly the same, in ways that relate, at least in my mind, directly to college basketball.

The most interesting aspect of *Duel* is its illumination of relatively early roots in America of basic political differences that exist to this day. To the real scholars out there this will seem rudimentary, incomplete and, I'm sure, inaccurate. With due apologies, I think *Duel* does a pretty nice job in capturing the essential fault lines between the Federalists, ancestors to today's Republicans, led by Hamilton, and the ancestors of today's Democrats, which, just to make it more confusing, were then known as Republicans, led by Thomas Jefferson.

I am interested in the subject matter, having finally slogged through the David McCullough biography on John Adams this summer. The Adams book provides a context that *Duel* lacks, with a very good discussion of the international aspects of the era and particularly the critical influence not only of the British, but also the French, on the political development of the infant American nation. The Federalists tilt to England, toward a political and economic elite, and, it was argued, toward favoring not just aristocracy but also monarchy if not dictatorship. There is a high value on order and on certainty, lest civilization collapse into the chaos, disorder and violence embodied by the Jacobins and the Reign of Terror. The Jefferson Republicans, by contrast, rejoiced in the French Revolution, the Age of Enlightenment and the view that "all men are created equal" (so long as they are white and not women, but that's a story for another day). Hamilton repeatedly is accused of attempting to become the American Bonaparte, of trying to replace the English Monarchy, from which the young country had broken, with a monarchy or a dictatorship controlled by him.

I would submit to you that these essential fault lines: the elite vs. the people; equality vs. advantages of birth, talent or achievement; liberty and freedom vs. law and order, run deep throughout our history and indeed the history of the world, and that the reason is that these tensions exist in all of us. As they say, much of where you stand depends upon where you sit. Or in basketball terms, from a Pitt fan's perspective, Duke has unfair advantages and Duquesne has nothing to complain about.

****

So, having provided a seventh grade level "history" of post-Revolutionary America, only one question remains: What in the world did this gift have to do with basketball? The answer, of course, is everything.

It is not, at least to my knowledge, that uber-referee Jim Burr is a descendent of Aaron Burr, although the vice president's nickname, the Colonel, surely would befit our modern Burr, and I shall henceforth refer to him as such.

Instead, it is Pitt basketball. A few years ago, my family and I used to laugh and laugh at a television commercial. It was one of the early "Got Milk" commercials. In the commercial, a classical music radio station was giving away $10,000 to the first caller who could name the man who killed Alexander Hamilton in a duel. The star of the commercial knows the answer (his room is filled with "memorabilia" of the event) but he has a mouthful of peanut butter and all he can say into the phone, over and over, is an indecipherable "AAAAArrrwwiiN BBBBBRRRR."

And so, of course, from the day he got here, we have met every good play by our now almost All-American center with a garbled but joyful cheer:

"AAAARRWWWIIINNN GGGWWWWAAAAYYY!!!!"

Moreover, this same essential fault line that existed at the birth of the republic also has existed for as long as I can remember in college basketball. The need for certainty, for order, for an elite, versus the self-evident truth that all teams are created equal. In my youth, there was UCLA, a kind of George Washington, not perfect and perhaps open to some historical re-thinking, but something of a benevolent king, which brought a consistent excellence to the game unmatched before or since. Lesser royalty, but royalty nonetheless, in North Carolina and Kentucky, royalty whose status has passed from generation to generation. We have survived a potential Bonaparte, Knight of Indiana.

But for going on 20 years, the embodiment of college basketball royalty has been Duke and its somewhat unlikely-looking historical figure, Coach K. It is, always, an annoying type of royalty, with its own TV network, ESPN, and propaganda ministry, Vitale, Patrick and Feinstein. It can be more than annoying, such as last week when Duke won two games by three points while shooting 80 foul shots to 24 for Boston College and Florida State.

For those who believe that all men are created equal, that a foul on Craig Smith is a foul on Shelden Williams, this is unacceptable. If, though, as I believe, there always will be some tilt toward royalty, including in basketball, we could do a lot worse than Duke. And it's not because they are benevolent, because they aren't, or that they set a standard of excellence, because they don't. It is because, if I can share a deep, dark secret, DUKE IS NOT THAT GOOD.

Since 1992, Duke has won one national championship. UConn has won two in the past seven years. UCLA won 10 in 12 years. Duke has been to four Final Fours in the past 13 years. Michigan State has been to four Final Fours in the past seven years. Duke is not good enough to win this year without the tilting of the playing field that royalty demands. And yet, year after year, Duke is treated as if it stands alone atop college basketball.

So, if our nature demands royalty, Duke it shall be. Perhaps the next iteration will be worse.

Burr is portrayed in *Duel* as the original American moderate, a schemer (like Hamilton, and Jefferson, if you believe the author) with a foot in each camp. At this stage of my reading, the political rivalry and the immediate issue, control of the governorship of New York, have been framed. The events that lead to the duel are starting to come clear. But I know how it ends, who gets to shoot and who gets shot.

Not unlike a Duke game.

17-15

FEBRUARY 5, 2006	GEORGETOWN 61 PITT 58
FEBRUARY 9, 2006	PITT 57 WVU 53
FEBRUARY 12, 2006	PITT 89 CINCINNATI 69
FEBRUARY 15, 2006	PITT 85 @ PROVIDENCE 77

Pitt recruited two very good college centers in 2003, Chris Taft and Aaron Gray. Many Pitt "fans" criticized Taft because all he did was dunk and then they criticized Gray because he did not dunk every time. After Aaron shot nine for nine from the field at Providence, it was time to acknowledge his remarkable progress.

In other news, Vice President Cheney shot somebody.

In a Big Country, Dreams Stay With You   Posted on 2/17/06

I spent time this week, as I assume most people did, watching tapes of the 1995 NCAA Basketball Tournament to see what the future might hold for our 2006 Pittsburgh Panthers.

On a tip from a friend, we attended the first round games in the 1995 tournament in Baltimore as proud members of the Retrievers Club of the University of Maryland, Baltimore County. As a $25 donor, I was able to purchase six tickets, lower level, between the baselines. I believe that it is the best $25 I have ever spent, although I need to be careful because I am not sure how much our marriage license cost.

I have several memories from this tournament, most of them

CARL AND THE BIG WHITE BOYS

wonderful. There is very little better on this earth than having your six-year-old son on your lap as his "man," Antonio McDyess, went off for 39 in a classic overtime game against a Penn team with a fabulous pair of guards, Jerome Allen and Matt Maloney. For all of the basketball I have watched, as a non-NBA fan in a non-NBA town, it is notable how few of the greatest players I have seen in person. Tim Duncan was in Baltimore, he was a sophomore and there was no question, not for a minute, that he was such a player. I also remember running into my friend, who had been with us in Baltimore that summer, and he laughed and said: "Did you see our hotel on *60 Minutes?* It was featured as the murder capital of the United States."

While my wife and our eight- and ten-year-old daughters walked the streets of Baltimore at ten at night to go back to the Murder Hotel, I stayed at the arena because my six-year-old son had told me "I want to see Big Country."

Which, of course, is why I was watching this tape. Bryant Reeves, Big Country, took Oklahoma State to the Final Four, and to do it he went through McDyess and Duncan and Marcus Camby, probably all of whom, and certainly Duncan, are better than any player Aaron Gray will have to play as he attempts to lead Pitt to the Final Four. Big Country did this with a supporting cast that included a fine college guard, Randy Rutherford, roughly comparable to Carl, a pretty good point

WE ALL WE GOT

guard, Andre Owens, and some eminently forgettable players.

Aaron Gray is very much in Big Country's class as a college player. Big Country was heavier, about 290. He had one thing that Aaron does not have: a go-to turnaround jumper. But if anything, Aaron moves a little better and has a more complete game, and he clearly is a better rebounder than Big Country was. You could quibble either way, but these are similar players and if Big Country was good enough to take that supporting cast to the Final Four, Aaron Gray can take this one.

****

But Oklahoma State had one thing that Pitt does not quite have, at least not this year or at least not yet. The way I would describe it is "two hands, two feet." Crisp passes with two hands from a solid base with two feet firmly on the ground. Sharp cuts. Playing through contact. Two hands, two feet, on balance, in your stance on defense. Grinding teams down, making everything an effort against you, every basket and every stop earned. So that when Alabama was up 24-15 on Oklahoma State in the middle of the first half I could turn to my friend and say that this game was over, that Oklahoma State had them, and be certain that it was so.

It is not the only way to play. You can win with overwhelming talent played at a high tempo, like North Carolina last year, or UConn two years ago or some of the Kentucky or Arizona or UNLV teams. Or you can win, at least to a point, with finesse, like WVU these days or the old Princeton teams. Or with something truly unique, like the Paul Westhead teams at Loyola Marymount, or maybe Villanova this year. I appreciate all of these styles and love some of them.

I like the flashy play more than almost anyone. If I could add two tapes to my collection it would be the 1973 Final Four with Ernie D. against Memphis State and the game in the 1986 tournament when Scott Skiles shut up Georgetown with one wrap-around pass. We could debate the appropriate level of contact. But as I get older and stodgier I am increasingly of the view that there is a word for the way UCLA played in 1973 and Oklahoma State played in 1995, the way Michigan State has often played under Izzo and Utah played under Majerus and how Pitt played for three years and almost is playing now and might still play.

Basketball.

17-15

FEBRUARY 18, 2006 | MARQUETTE 84 PITT 82

After a tough loss at Marquette, Pitt came home to play Providence and celebrate the 100th year of Pitt basketball, and to honor the three remaining members of Pitt's only Final Four team, from 1941. This one went to a good friend and did not go to the Board.

2/25/06

In case you haven't seen it yet, there is an excellent story in today's *Post-Gazette* about Pitt's 1941 Final Four team, along with a team picture. I have a post-script to this story that I thought you would enjoy.

About 15 years ago, my wife bought me a t-shirt with that same picture as a gift. I looked at it and did a double-take. In the front row, second from the left, wearing Number 5, was Dr. Mendel "Red" Silverman. I knew it was him because he looked exactly like his son Ronny, with whom I had played a lot of pick-up basketball as a kid. I also was vaguely aware that Dr. Silverman had played a little basketball at Pitt a long time ago.

I would say that Dr. Silverman was a friend but that would not do him justice. When I was a child, he was my pediatrician. He was my wife's pediatrician too, even though we did not know each other growing up. Then he was our kids' pediatrician. Dr. Red, as we called him because of his bright red hair, was the kind of doctor that you don't see very often anymore, the kind who would come to your house in the middle of the night. Throughout the 1980s and 1990s, when we took the kids to his office, or even when we didn't, I would get my allergy shots with him and we would visit every week, usually about what was going on with the Pitt basketball or football teams. He had hundreds of pictures on the wall of children he had taken care of over the years. He lived modestly but well, and he walked to work every day until about five years ago when he died one Saturday afternoon at the age of eighty after having worked that morning. I miss him and think of him often to this day.

Of course, when we got it, we showed him the t-shirt with the team picture. He was very excited to tell me about that team and all the fine players on it, emphasizing as was his nature that he was only a reserve. He and his wife went out and bought shirts for all of their children, two of whom also became doctors, and for their grandchildren.

I am told by my father-in-law, who grew up with him, that Dr. Red was an excellent basketball player, even if he only was a benchwarmer on the 1941 Final Four team. After that year, I believe, he left the team to concentrate on becoming a doctor. Although there were many better players on that team, and I am sure many fine men, it is difficult to imagine that the 1941 Pitt Panthers produced a better man than Dr. Red Silverman.

Best regards.

FEBRUARY 25, 2006	PITT 81 PROVIDENCE 68
FEBRUARY 27, 2006	WEST VIRGINIA 67 PITT 62
MARCH 3, 2006	SETON HALL 65 @ PITT 61

This one is pretty self-explanatory. The Seton Hall loss was particularly painful because it was Senior Night for Carl and because they had been undefeated at home until then.

March   Posted on 3/5/06

I am grateful to this team. It is March and they have helped to get me through another long winter. I am concerned that after their months of hard and fine work, all they have done is set themselves up for criticism from the great unwashed if they end up playing like most people had thought they would play all along.

With this in mind, I did some tossing and turning after the West Virginia game. It is hard to pinpoint, but there was something different about that loss. Maybe it was the subtle change in the rotation—Graves ahead of Benjamin, the stress that showed on Jamie, the way Carl was pressing and a little sense of fatigue with Aaron, but there was a feeling that the delicate balance had been altered, that the karma was out of balance. They seem to be fighting the game right now.

It is a long year. Hopefully, there still is a lot of basketball left to play. At this point last year, Pitt had just finished a week with two extremely impressive road wins at Boston College and Notre Dame. Who would have guessed that all that was left of the season were two bad losses?

I just want them to play well and have fun, and not fight it, so that they leave with the memories they deserve, to go along with the memories they already have given all of us.

17-15

This one also did not go on the Board.

Senior Day   3/7/06

In November 2001, my son and I went, as we always did, to the Blue-Gold intrasquad scrimmage, to witness the birth of a new Pitt basketball season. Our expectations were on the low side, even after a surprise run to the Big East finals that March. We went because we always went. It was just one of the things we did.

We sat by ourselves in the bleachers at center court at the Field House, across from our regular seats. There were not many people there.

But after the Blue-Gold scrimmage of 2001, we both had a pretty good idea. For a while it was our secret.

The secret started to seep out when they went to Columbus and beat a good Ohio State team. 22-7, at least. Then we went for a ride. We would count it down together after every game. 20 and f—ing 4, 22 and f—ing 4. Calling him from London in the middle of the night to find out that Pitt won at Seton Hall in overtime, his little league coach bringing Billy Knight over to take a picture at the last game at the Field House, the night they went 25 and f—ing 4. To the Big East. To Mellon Arena. To Lexington. So drained when they lost that it almost was a relief.

We see them at the games sometimes but in a real sense they are all gone now. Mark. Yuri. Chad. Torrie. Ontario. Donatas. Julius. Chevy. Jaron. Brandin. It all seems like a long time ago, and they are all gone.

Except one.

The Blue-Gold scrimmage of 2001 was the first time we saw Carl Krauser play basketball. It would be a year until we saw him play again. It was exciting, in fact it was thrilling, the thought of adding Carl to the team that was unfolding before us. With Carl leading cheers in his Number 27 Eddie George jersey.

I would like to say that it stayed that way. In time, though, we didn't agree on Carl. We debated this, a lot, argued about it. It became clear, of course, that we were arguing about more than Carl Krauser. While we were off doing what fathers and teenage sons often need to do, Carl was on his own journey. Carl came here as a boy and he is leaving here a man, an old man if you believe the stock phrases that always are used with Carl. But his most special quality, the one I will remember, is that, in the best sense, he has never grown up.

Many years ago, before any of our children were born, I went to see *E.T.* with my wife and my late brother. When it was over, I said that I had enjoyed it but I did not understand what all the fuss was about. My brother, who was an artist, said, no, that was the most powerful movie he had ever seen; that it was about the things you feel as a child and how they sustain you your whole life.

If *E.T.* had been about Carl, I would have gotten it.

For all his talents and even for his flaws, the thing that I will remember most about Carl is that he never lost the youthful joy of playing basketball and that he sucked the juice out of that experience better than any player I can ever remember.

I cherish the time I have spent watching Pitt basketball with my son, the time we still spend. I will miss him terribly when he is away at school next year. Like Carl, I hope he never loses the little boy in him.

But he's growing up. I am learning, not always fast enough, that when your kids grow up, they grow up. They have their own ideas and their own opinions. I'm not sure, exactly, where my son ended up on Carl. I am sure it is fair. This much I know. When he is old and gray, he will remember Carl. We all will.

Some people are just unforgettable.

Goodbye Carl. Thank you. And God bless.

MARCH 8, 2006	PITT 61 LOUISVILLE 56
	[BIG EAST TOURNAMENT]
MARCH 9, 2006	PITT 68 WEST VIRGINIA 57
	[BIG EAST TOURNAMENT]
MARCH 10, 2006	PITT 68 VILLANOVA 54
	[BIG EAST TOURNAMENT]

My wife, our son and I went back to the Big East after all. Every day it felt a little more like we had turned the clock back four years.

Sweet Dreams   Posted on 3/11/06

In New York. 3:16 a.m. Saturday morning. Pinch me if this is real:

With no warning, Pitt has played like a Final Four team from the moment they got here. As our older daughter text-messaged my wife during the first 17 minutes against Louisville, after Pitt went up 35-7: "I'm glad they had their little talk."

Last week Pitt looked like a one and done team. Maybe they will look that way again next week. I doubt it. Even if they do, they are having the moment they deserve.

During the 2002 Big East Tournament, one of the New York writers wrote, as I recall it: "There is no secret why Pitt is winning. They have good players and lots of them." Pitt is overwhelming teams again, with good players and lots of them, players whose talents have been nurtured and blended over the whole season and in some cases over many seasons. By a coach and a staff who see the good in players and what they can be. Players who are playing like they understand that there is a tiny window in life to do something like this and that very few people ever get the chance

Which is why they just dismantled the Number 2 team in the country.

The Big East Tournament is a big deal. It might be the biggest deal, really. If Pitt can hold off Gerry Awe-Inspiring-Un-Freakin'-Believable McNamara and Syracuse's suddenly stirring big men, and I think they will, and if that's their moment, or if tonight and last night was their moment, it will be theirs to treasure and ours to savor.

But I don't think it ends there. Pitt is starting to run downhill. They have started to visualize what they can be.

17-15

MARCH 11, 2006	SYRACUSE 65 PITT 61 [BIG EAST FINALS]
MARCH 17, 2006	PITT 79 KENT STATE 64 [NCAA TOURNAMENT]
MARCH 19, 2006	BRADLEY 72 PITT 66 [NCAA TOURNAMENT]

2005-2006 RECORD: 25-8

Actually, by the end, Florida didn't have any flaws.

That's It, Good Season   Posted on 3/23/06

It all fit.

After watching Pitt in the Big East Tournament, I really thought that they could go to the Final Four. Some of that was active self-delusion. But, in fairness:

I knew that Pitt had real flaws. Every team in this tournament has flaws. College basketball isn't what it once was, and even by modern standards, it's a bit of a down year.

My comment to my wife in New York was that there were modestly flawed teams, seriously flawed teams and deeply flawed teams, and Pitt was in a relatively small group of teams that were modestly flawed. Somebody is going to win the tournament, and I did not see a team that was clearly better than the Pitt team that played in New York. Still don't.

So, it was not all self-delusion.

But some of it was. And I would not give that up for anything. Within limits, I will define my own experience here. In a small way, often an unhealthy way, I take the journey with them every year; I live and die with them, I share their hopes and dreams, and I believe that anything is possible until it isn't. Then I start all over again. That's the way that I want it to stay.

I want to be inspired.

Pitt inspired me up in New York. From the opening tip of the Louisville game to the final buzzer of the Syracuse game, Pitt was a TEAM. When they played well, they played as a team. But, more important, even in the rough stretches, they played as a team. When they lost to Syracuse, they lost as a team.

It continued with a superb performance against Kent State. With Aaron Gray, the most important piece of the puzzle, the young man whose work ethic and development made all things possible, a development that was never enough for a large portion of "fans" who rarely missed an opportunity to display their complete ignorance, looking rejuvenated after a draining season, a season with far more minutes than he had ever played, tough minutes in the post, an even more draining Big East Tournament, and a bout with the flu.

The whole was greater than the parts. Every player had a role. It all fit.

And then it didn't fit.

Just like that. It happens. All credit to Bradley. They rattled Pitt early in that game. One of the highest compliments I can pay this Pitt team is that I finally reached the point that it was beneath their dignity for me to fixate on the referees. I thought that Pitt being in early foul trouble against Bradley was a symptom of Bradley taking them out of their game, not the cause.

Yet, by halftime, I was optimistic. Even though they had done it with a patchwork line-up and less well-oiled teamwork than in New York, I thought Pitt had weathered the storm, taken Bradley's best shot, whatever other cliché you can think of. That's how the second half started.

Then Carl missed a quick three-pointer that I thought was neither a great nor a terrible idea. A couple minutes later, Aaron Gray took a technical foul, showing a frustration that was completely unexpected and out of character, a frustration that I am inclined to think also was more a symptom than a cause, although I am not sure what triggered it, and the karma broke and the wheels fell off and even for the team that NEVER quit, not once, there was not quite enough time to put them back on. When all was said and done, this team had great heart, led by the King of Heart, Carl Krauser, the kind of heart that doesn't let you lose a game by double figures in two years, and only one in three years, but, in my opinion, with the notable exception of Kendall and maybe one or two others, it just did not quite have the emotional maturity to carry it off. Give Bradley this. When the opportunity arose, when Pitt cracked for just a moment, Bradley did not waste one second in re-taking control of the game. There is not a question in my mind that the right team won that game.

****

And that's OK.

These are children, really, about the same ages as my own children. I think about my own emotional maturity just watching these games, not to mention in the real world, and it is lacking many times. Reading this Board, especially after a loss, I feel safe in saying that I am not alone. Sure, you'd like them to lose at their very best, to feel that they had taken it as far as it could possibly go, the way West Virginia did against Louisville last year. Yes, it was a missed opportunity to raise the profile of the program.

It happens. And it's OK.

Seeing the tape of Antonio Graves in tears on the way to the locker room after shooting 0-8 when he had played so well in New York will stay with me. As will the picture of Aaron Gray slumped in his locker, looking almost small but not diminished, plastered by *One of America's Great Newspapers* across a front page rarely visited by Pitt basketball. A part of that feeling probably will stay with them. But I am confident that, in time, they will come to understand that being so committed to something larger than themselves, being willing to take the chance when the risk of failure is real and painful and public, being IN IT, is the most important part of the experience, and a big part of growing up.

Of all people, Carl Krauser seems to understand this, deeply, at least after the game, and in his own way he is very articulate on the subject. If only he could have found a way to bring the same perspective to the court without losing the single-minded, never give one inch, "I can fix this" drive, that at the same time was his, and Pitt's, greatest strength and occasional downfall.

That, and to know what it feels like to really come together as a team, as they did for four glorious days in New York, even if they were not quite able to hold it together. This team deserved to have their moment, and in my eyes they had it.

It would be great to see them have a magical NCAA Tournament run some year. But as I think about it, watching them put it on the line every night for five months, watching them grow up, watching them become a team, is plenty inspiring enough for me.

It's been another great season.

And I am sure that next year will be even better. I always am.

17-15

CHAPTER SIX

"ONCE MORE INTO THE BREACH"

With Carl gone, it looked like Pitt was heading for a rebuilding year. Then Aaron Gray decided to come back for his senior year.

The Positive Choice

Posted on 6/23/06

Aaron Gray is, at the least and very possibly the most, a classic NBA back-up center. He should earn a very good living for a long time. He never will be Russell or Chamberlain. Nobody would have begrudged him taking the safe road and the easier road and getting started on that now. But he didn't and I am very proud of him. Not for the glory of old State U and blah, blah, blah, although I hope that part of the reason he is coming back is that he understands something my father told me when I was six years old that gets more painfully true every year: "You are only young once."

No, I am proud of Aaron Gray because he chose the road that was harder and not as safe. The road that gives him the best chance of being the best basketball player and maybe even the best person he can be—not that it is any of my business.

Aaron Gray just has not played that much basketball at a high level, really only last year. He needs more time in the center of the action, not at the end of an NBA bench. More time in situations that develop maturity in a young player. More time to be The Man.

When you are The Man in college basketball, you are asking to fail. There is almost no possible result this coming season that won't be a disappointment. As The Man, and especially with the type of player he is, Aaron will come in for special criticism. Two years ago, Aaron averaged four points a game. This year he will he criticized by many and vilified by some if he doesn't lead Pitt—a team that does not have a single player recruited by North Carolina, Duke or Kansas, a team playing without Brandin Knight or Carl Krauser for the first time in this century—to the Final Four or at least the Elite Eight.

Welcome back, Aaron. I hope you have the season that you deserve.

17-15

With Aaron Gray back, Pitt opened the 2006-2007 season with almost exactly the same team, except, importantly, Carl Krauser was gone. But Mike Cook, a 6-3 swingman from Philadelphia, was eligible after transferring from East Carolina, where he had averaged 15 points a game in a good conference. This also was the season that Brandin Knight returned to join the coaching staff after suffering a serious leg injury that ended his career as a player. All of which combined to make Pitt a preseason Top 10 team and brought with it an even louder chorus that the only thing that would define the 2006-2007 team would be whether it broke through the Sweet Sixteen.

There had been a stunning tragedy in the off-season. Jamie Dixon's 28-year-old sister Maggie, who had coached Army's women's team to the NCAA tournament only weeks before, died suddenly of a heart arrhythmia. The season began with an emotional and impressive win over Western Michigan in the first Maggie Dixon Classic, at West Point. Pitt would win its first ten games, including an annihilation of Florida State in which Pitt led by 36 before calling off the dogs, and a road win at Auburn. Yet even as Pitt rose to Number 2 in the country, something was missing.

Fool's Gold

Resolve. Focus. Teamwork. Mental Toughness. Accountability. Defense.

Pitt Defense.

The kind of defense that holds a UConn team with Caron Butler, Emeka Okafor and Ben Gordon to 52 points in regulation.

This is a much more elegant offensive basketball team than we are used to seeing. It opens up possibilities. But it isn't going to be worth a whit if this team doesn't play Pitt Defense.

It is early in the season. That's what Jamie says and, to a point, I think he's right. But it's early for Wisconsin, and for UCLA, and they are playing it.

It's not horrible. In fact, it's better than most.

But it's not Pitt Defense. In truth, it hasn't been for a couple of years. And if you can't keep your man in front of you against Robert Morris, how can you expect to do it against Florida and Kansas and North Carolina and Ohio State.

Pitt Defense. I'm like Justice Stewart. I know it when I see it.

This team can be really, really good. But if it isn't there by the end of the year, all that elegant offense will be so much fool's gold.

17-15

DECEMBER 16, 2006	WISCONSIN 89 PITT 75
DECEMBER 21, 2006	OKLAHOMA STATE 95 PITT 89 (2 OT)
DECEMBER 23, 2006	PITT 84 DAYTON 54
JANUARY 4, 2007	PITT 74 @ SYRACUSE 66
JANUARY 7, 2007	PITT 69 SOUTH FLORIDA 48
JANUARY 10, 2007	PITT 59 @ DEPAUL 49

The defensive chickens came home to roost against an excellent Wisconsin team in Madison, a game we attended with our son, a freshman there, our older daughter, up from Chicago, a cousin also in school there, and an old friend and summer basketball coach I had not seen since 1972. And, to a point, again at Oklahoma State in Oklahoma City the next week. The root of the problem was that, for a Top 10 team, and an excellent team in many ways, Pitt just was not that athletic. But they were working on their weaknesses, and they were making progress, including three blow-outs at home and good road wins at Syracuse and DePaul. Pitt was 15-2. With big games coming up against Georgetown, UConn and Marquette, home games I predicted they would win, it was a good time to take stock.

Midseason Report   Posted on 2/13/08

Here is a mid-season review of our nine man rotation. I will dispense with the letter grades that are customary in such analyses.

9. Tyrell Biggs. Reading this Board, I often feel like Mr. Opposite. To me, Biggs is a half-step away from really helping this team. He knows what they are trying to do but often he can't quite get there. He will. Any kid that loses 60 pounds is really working at it. Give this kid some time.

8. Sam Young. He is an enormous X factor on this team and a mystery to me. Maybe the best way to sum up Sam's season is to call the first half of the year a do-over. He has been hurt and he simply is not a small forward, where he spent a lot of time in November and December. Sam Young is just a sophomore and his game suggests that he has played most of it on a playground. I would like to counsel patience. But he can, and he must, be a key inside reserve for this team to realize its hopes and dreams. On a team that might be one athlete short, he could be that athlete.

7. Unless it's Keith Benjamin. This team started to make sense when Young went back to the power forward and Benjamin started getting minutes at the small forward. And what an athlete, even if he still looks more like a football athlete to me. If they want to be another tough Pitt team, they need players who are Pitt tough: Keith Benjamin.

6. Ronald Ramon. Sweet Ronald Ramon. The baby-faced assassin. Or as Rick Majerus called him, Ramone Raymond. And then "as good as any shooter in the gym." His defensive

fundamentals, like the rest of his game, are pure. Not very tall or quick, but many nights he sits down in that perfect stance and shuts down players who are far quicker. A fundamentally sound point guard, but not a great ball handler. Grown up enough to come off the bench when he could be starting, as he used to. And always as good as any shooter in the gym. You are not going to zone the Pitt Panthers as long as we have Ramone Raymond on our team.

5. Mike Cook. Maybe the best way to appreciate the way Pitt has played basketball the past six years is to watch a player who learned a different way. Mike Cook is the most talented offensive wing player Pitt has had in that entire period. He can shoot. He can dribble. He can pass. He can drive. He can, as they used to say, hang in the air. He can post up. He is a world class cherry picker, usually in a good way. He may never be Jaron on defense or on the boards, but he has improved. If he can keep unlearning the habits he picked up along the way, and define himself only by winning, he can be a great player on this team.

4. Levon Kendall. The Glue. Heady, steady, gutty, does all the little things. We have heard it about every white role player for the past thirty years. It's the most transparent and insidious form of racism, and we hear it about Kendall over and over again.

WE ALL WE GOT

But here's the thing. With Kendall, IT'S TRUE. Pitt has had a lot of exceptional basketball players over the past six years, players who made each other better. But for making the other players around them better, to my lights, there are three players who stand above the crowd: Brandin Knight, Jaron Brown and Levon Kendall. Kendall is not the all-around player that Brandin and Jaron were, but on defense, he has a complete understanding of what Pitt is trying to do and constantly helps and directs his teammates. On offense, and this will sound even more clichéd, he has a musician's sense of pace. Levon Kendall is the kind of player who makes teams win, and he can play on my team any day.

3. Antonio Graves. Another basketball cliché is "playing like a senior." Sometimes it's true too, and it's true with Antonio Graves. If Kendall has a musician's feel for the game, Graves, well, doesn't. He often makes up his mind very early if he is going to shoot or pass and his solution to most problems is to go faster and try harder.

I am more than content to take the bad with the good. After that tribute to Levon, it is high praise indeed to put Antonio in the third slot. He's earned that, with defense and perseverance and—unlike Kendall—scoring, which still is the object of the game.

2. Levance Fields. Also modestly recruited, Levance has been a triumph for the Pitt staff. As a sophomore, the second most important player on a Top 10 team. The natural leader of the team, by temperament and position. He may not be the glue but in cliché-land he's the straw that stirs the drink.

1. Aaron Gray. Without him, it's a bubble team. With him, it's Number 7 in the country and looking like it belongs there. The issue with Gray is stamina. Last January, he dominated two number-one draft choices, Hilton Armstrong and Josh Boone, on the road at UConn, with 23 points and 12 rebounds. By March, though, he was very low on gas. Nobody has done more work on his game or his conditioning. We will just have to see if it holds up.

So that's our team. But no midseason review would be complete without talking about the job that Jamie Dixon and his staff have done. They have recognized their weaknesses, rebounding and defense, which is easy, and have made progress, especially on defense, which is hard. So that if all the stars align and they can find that one last athlete, maybe it isn't even midseason yet.

17-15

JANUARY 13, 2007	PITT 74 GEORGETOWN 69
JANUARY 16, 2007	PITT 63 UCONN 54
JANUARY 21, 2007	MARQUETTE 77 @ PITT 74 (OT)

Before a national ESPN Gameday audience on a Saturday night, Pitt beat Georgetown in a game in which both teams played exceptionally well. Pitt then beat the first UConn team in memory that was not really UCONN, the Huskies having lost their top six players, four to the first round of the NBA draft. Then, with an opportunity to seize control of the Big East, Pitt stumbled at home against Marquette. Pitt was OK at 17-3 but they had missed a chance. They had an urgent need to develop a reliable inside sub and had to decide whether it was Sam Young or Tyrell Biggs.

The Third Man   Posted on 1/23/07

The version with Joseph Cotten and Orson Welles. Not the version entitled "The Third Mouse" featured on *Pinky and the Brain,* a show that is the source of a recurring conversation with my younger daughter that never fails to make me laugh: "What are you doing tonight, dear?" "Same thing we do every night: Try to take over the world." Even if that version would be more apt for the many people here who desire, no, demand, nothing less than that Pitt take over the world.

I am not giving in to the "take over the world" crowd. For me, the standard never changes: the best team they can be. A lot needs to happen to reach that standard. Issue number one is to find The Third Man to support Gray and Kendall. And a delicate process it will be.

The Third Man contains this famous speech: "In Italy, for thirty years under the Borgias, they had warfare, terror, murder, bloodshed — they produced Michelangelo, Leonardo da Vinci and the Renaissance. In Switzerland, they had brotherly love, five hundred years of democracy and peace, and what did that produce? The cuckoo clock."

I would bet that Jamie chooses brotherly love and peace and plays them both. But they need at least one. Or, they could just play Gray and Kendall until they drop.

17-15

Another post inspired by our younger daughter, who never ceases to broaden and brighten our world. She is interested in everything, and she brings us along. As here, when she brought over a fascinating movie about a different kind of gift that, in my mind, was part of a common thread.

Why We Care   Posted on 2/3/07

To see people be the best they ever will be.

Doing what they were born to do.

Doing what they love.

Doing what we love.

Doing things we dream of doing.

Doing things we can only dream of doing.

With other people just like them.

Or almost just like them.

Passion.

Preparation.

Concentration.

One chance for perfection.

Under pressure.

On the biggest stage.

A crowd of people.

People who marvel at them.

People who sort of understand.

And a few people who Know.

The difference between a talent and a gift.

Between a gift and genius.

A chance that only comes once a year.

Where champions are remembered forever.

And the heartbreak of the tiniest error never fades.

Final Four?

Could be.

Could be a lot of things.

Ellen Ripstein. Al Sanders. Trip Payne. Tyler Hinman.

Will Shortz.

Wordplay.

"If you don't come across, I'm gonna be down."

17-15

JANUARY 24, 2007	PITT 67 @ CINCINNATI 51
JANUARY 27, 2007	PITT 72 ST. JOHN'S 46
JANUARY 29, 2007	PITT 65 @ VILLANOVA 59
FEBRUARY 7, 2007	PITT 60 @ WEST VIRGINIA 47

Back to basketball. Including a couple more impressive road wins at Villanova and West Virginia, a game in which Sam Young scored 21 points off the bench, taking over the game in the second half after I had used halftime to explain in detail to some friends all of Sam's supposed weaknesses. Pitt was 21-3. My imaginary friend DT posted that he saw The Look. My son saw it. I wanted to see it, too, in the worst way. But I didn't.

The Comfort Zone   Posted on 2/10/07

No matter how enjoyable, my favorite part of any trip is when I hit my own bed with my own pillow. It's just my comfort zone and as Walter Cronkite used to say: "All things are exactly as they were then."

As we reach the head of the stretch, I find myself back in the comfort zone with Pitt.

****

Pitt has reverted to Pitt tempo. Thank goodness. Pitt made West Virginia look like Eric Von Zipper, even if at times they made themselves look that way too.

Would Pitt really be able to slow down Florida or North Carolina? Probably not, but as Pitt showed at Wisconsin, they aren't likely just to outscore them either. I'll take their best chance to win and if it's not good enough, it's not good enough. Besides, that will just give some people something else to complain about...

****

The Usual Suspects are once again deeply immersed in the annual debate over what will cause Pitt to lose in the NCAA Tournament, an exercise akin to spending your whole life arguing about how you are going to die. Pitt very probably will lose someday and, when they do, be assured that the Usual Suspects will have told us so.

****

It's still a little early but I am starting to get that lump in my throat about college basketball that takes me back to when life was simple and pure. Bucky Waters was the announcer the other night at West Virginia. In the winter of 1966, when I was eight years old, I would go down to the basement of our old house where I could pull in a grainy version of Channel 7 on a little Philco and watch Ron Williams and Carl Head and West Virginia, coached by the same Bucky Waters, in a big Southern Conference game against Dick Snyder and Rodney Knowles and Davidson, coached by Lefty Driesell. I will be 50 next month and a not-so-small part of me would give anything to be eight years old and back in front of that little TV just one time.

****

So, as we reach the head of the stretch, all things are as they were then and I'm back in the comfort zone. I'm all in for our Panthers, as always. But, truth be told, I am not all the way there with them yet. It's a fine team, a really fine team and it is getting better. But, DT, I don't see The Look. Not yet. I want to, I do, and I am watching for it. But I don't see it yet.

Even The Look is no guaranty. My son and I each believe that Florida is one of the finest college basketball teams of the past 15-20 years, with exquisite balance and teamwork that is the antithesis of relying on a go-to guy. A 2002-2003 Pitt team but with NBA size and talent in the forecourt. Yet, in the single elimination world of college basketball, even Florida is no lock to make the Final Four, much less repeat as national champions.

So I'm not there yet, but I want to be. I want to think about why they might live, not how they might die. There is one more thing. I have received one text message in my life, from my son, during the Pitt-Dayton game in December. It carried a lot of meaning from a lot of years, even if it isn't where I am yet, and whether it turns out to be right or not.

"Dad, Pitt is a Final Four team."

17-15

FEBRUARY 10, 2007	PITT 74 PROVIDENCE 68
FEBRUARY 12, 2007	LOUISVILLE 66 @ PITT 53
FEBRUARY 17, 2007	PITT 65 WASHINGTON 61
FEBRUARY 19, 2007	PITT 71 @ SETON HALL 68

After getting by Providence, Pitt got waxed at home by Louisville in a way they had never been waxed in the five years at the Peterson Center. They bounced back against Washington, but Aaron Gray was hurt at the end of that game and was never really the same that season. With Gray out, Pitt managed to hold off Seton Hall in the Meadowlands, led by an impressive performance by Levon Kendall filling in at center and 15 second-half points by Levance Fields. Next, they had to go to Georgetown and its huge and talented front line with Gray on one leg if at all.

Heart   Posted on 2/24/07

It has been kind of a rough week. First, Aaron Gray went down with an ankle injury that is starting to sound like it might be the whole thing.

On Thursday, Dennis Johnson died of a heart attack. He was only a couple years older than I am. While he is best known for his years with the Celtics, what I remember best about Dennis Johnson was when he emerged to greatness on the 1978 Seattle Supersonics of Gus Williams, Downtown Freddie

Brown and DJ at guard, and Johnny Johnson, Jack Sikma and Marvin "The Human Eraser" Webster up front. In the spring of 1978, I worked outside of Morgantown. Every game, we would drive to Star City to watch the Sonics play the Bullets, with the Big E, Wes Unseld and Bobby Dandridge, on the big screen TV. In 180 playoff games, Dennis Johnson averaged over 17 points, had an assist-to-turnover ratio of over 2 to 1 and played Hall of Fame defense. Peace DJ.

Then to read on Thursday night a much smaller tragedy but one that will affect me more: Steve Rushin is leaving *Sports Illustrated* after 19 years. The best sportswriter of our generation in my view. Without him, I have precious little reason to read *Sports Illustrated,* as I have done every Thursday for the past 41 years. But I will.

Because the game goes on. It always does. Today, they get Georgetown, at Georgetown, either without Aaron Gray or with a shell of him, with Georgetown's greatest strength, Roy Hibbert and Jeff Green, right down Main Street where Aaron Gray would be.

Every Pitt team the past six years would show for this game. It might not win, but it would show, and it would make us proud.

This one will too.

17-15

FEBRUARY 24, 2007	GEORGETOWN 61 PITT 53
FEBRUARY 27, 2007	PITT 80 WEST VIRGINIA 66
MARCH 3, 2007	MARQUETTE 75 PITT 71

Pitt did show at Georgetown, rallying to take an eight-point lead in the middle of the second half. Gray played Hibbert to a draw while limping badly, a courageous performance that will be forgotten by most. But Jeff Green took over down the stretch, and Georgetown pulled away at the end, playing at a level Pitt could not match and that would propel them to the Final Four. Then, after a nice bounce-back win against West Virginia, Pitt faltered again at Marquette, a game we attended with all of our children to celebrate the sad and imminent occasion of my 50th birthday. Pitt did not look right and many of the most faithful, even DT, were discouraged.

The Month of Dreams   Posted on 3/6/07

This team has not played its best basketball yet.

This Board knows better.

Et tu, DT?

I am aware of the problems, and have been. Certainly they have been detailed here.

But this team has not played its best basketball yet.

Some of it is a wish because it is March, the month of dreams. A lot of it is a feeling, the rhythm of a basketball season that says that almost every team has its moment and this team has not had its yet.

At the end of the day it is an affair of the heart. On the way out of the Bradley Center on Saturday I asked my son if he was down. He said no, this team is good. It can do well. He has said this all year. If he is right, I am right with him. If he is wrong, I am right with him.

We win as a team. We lose as a team.

17-15

MARCH 8, 2007	PITT 89 MARQUETTE 79
	[BIG EAST TOURNAMENT]
MARCH 9, 2007	PITT 65 LOUISVILLE 59
	[BIG EAST TOURNAMENT]

The Big East Tournament. In this decade, the scene of the most stirring basketball that Pitt has ever played. As my son had assured me it would be, this was another chapter. With five players in double figures, led by Aaron Gray's 22, 17 from the Third Man, Sam Young, and 16 from a rejuvenated Mike Cook, Pitt soundly defeated a Marquette team that had beaten them twice. Then, down 11 at the half to a Louisville team that had embarrassed them in Pittsburgh, Pitt started the second half with a stunning 20-2 run led by Antonio Graves of Mansfield, Ohio, who finished with 23 points. Pitt held on after a remarkable game-saving play by Levon Kendall, who dove for an offensive rebound and, flat on his back, managed to get the ball out to Graves, who then put the game away with his fourth three-pointer of the half.

In a league with tradition-steeped programs like UConn, Syracuse, Georgetown, Villanova, Louisville, Marquette and St. John's, Pitt was in the finals of the Big East Tournament for the sixth time in seven years.

Smile

The movie *Diner* begins with one of my favorite characters, Timothy Fenwick, played by Kevin Bacon, breaking windows in the basement of what appears to be a high school. When Boogie Sheftel, played by Mickey Rourke, asks him why, he tells him, "It's a smile."

One of the great smiles, that of Antonio Graves, is lighting up the world this morning. It often does. As a father of children about his age, I found it heartwarming, truly, to see Antonio beaming with his family on Senior Night. A quick story, relayed to my wife at the game last night by an elderly couple: At breakfast yesterday morning, this gentleman had come up to Antonio and said, "Young man, you and I have something in common." "What is that, sir?" "Many years ago I got my pilot's license, and when I did my first flight, I landed in Mansfield, Ohio." With that, Antonio Graves lit up and asked the couple if they could take a picture together and the next thing you know they were surrounded by the entire team for a group picture.

Antonio has a lot to smile about this morning. He played one memorable basketball game last night. He was not alone. There were many heroes, none bigger than Antonio—unless it was Levon Kendall, who made many huge plays but one that ranks right up there with Brandin stealing that inbound pass as the greatest play Pitt ever has made in the Garden. Except this one won them the game. At least it did when Antonio finished it with a three-pointer that was even more important than the three of them he drilled to start the second half.

I would be remiss if I failed to mention the superb play of Mike Cook in this tournament.

We hear a lot about what Pitt does not have. True enough. But today would be a good day to talk about what Pitt does have: Experience. Depth. Adaptability.

Heart.

In this tournament, Pitt has gotten important contributions from all nine of its players. The nature of this team is that it is not always the same pistons firing.

Tonight, when Pitt stamps itself as the team of the decade in the Big East, I look for these pistons to be firing: Aaron Gray, Levance Fields and Ronald Ramon.

It'll be the smile of the week.

17-15

MARCH 10, 2007	GEORGETOWN 65 PITT 42
	[BIG EAST FINALS]
MARCH 15, 2007	PITT 79 WRIGHT ST. 58
	[NCAA TOURNAMENT]
MARCH 17, 2007	PITT 84 VIRGINIA COMMONWEALTH 79 (OT)
	[NCAA TOURNAMENT]

Pitt did not beat Georgetown; in fact they were slaughtered, inexplicably, and Roy Hibbert badly outplayed Aaron Gray, which he had never done before. Georgetown was very good, and it was growing in a way that Pitt did not seem to be. Still, Pitt was 27-7 and had just beaten two NCAA teams on a neutral court. Then, for once, Pitt got a fair seed in the NCAA Tournament, a third seed in Buffalo. It appeared they would finally play Duke, but, with a big lead, Duke collapsed under the pressure of a small but exceptionally quick and feisty Virginia Commonwealth team. On Saturday, after Pitt lost a 19-point lead and Levance Fields missed two foul shots with two seconds to go, it looked like the same thing would happen to Pitt. But it didn't.

Buffalo   Posted on 3/21/07

I had seen this game before. Coppin State - Texas in 1997 at the Civic Arena, with Antoine Brockington playing the role of Eric Maynor and Terquin Mott playing the part of Jesse Pellot-Rosa. I can only say that it was more fun being on the other side. And that the result was the same. And that a lot more people remember Coppin State than Texas, which is somewhat fitting for our anonymous Panthers.

Saturday's unfolding drama also brought to mind a memorable game from the 1970s. The game was Louisville against UCLA in the 1975 national semifinals, described by John Wooden as perhaps the greatest game in which he ever was involved. UCLA was led by David Meyers, Richard Washington, Marques Johnson, Andre McCarter and Pete Trgovich. Louisville was led by Junior Bridgeman, Allen Murphy and Wesley Cox. It also featured a classic match-up of teacher and pupil, Wooden and Denny Crum.

It was a taut game from wire to wire and UCLA ultimately survived in overtime, 75-74. For all of the great players, great plays and great coaches, though, the game is remembered, almost singly, for the one-on-one free throw missed by Terry Howard of Louisville that could have put the game away. This allowed the retiring Wooden the final championship he would go on to win and also denied Louisville the chance to play Kentucky, which had avoided them since 1959, in the national championship game. It was all the more painful because Terry Howard had not missed a free throw the entire season, having made 28 of 28 to that point.

Terry Howard has had to live with that for 32 years now. It could have been Levance Fields on Saturday, and really all of them. That would not have done justice to VCU and their stirring comeback. Or to the superb play that got Pitt the big lead, and even some fine plays down the stretch, or the adversity under which Pitt was playing. It would not have been fair. But that's just the way it is and I was heartsick at the prospect.

In the movies, the last shot always goes in. But these young people risk failure every single time out. The more they succeed, the bigger the stakes and the more lasting and painful the failure can be.

So they should at least be allowed to celebrate their accomplishments. This Pitt team is 29-7. It has done this with one possible NBA prospect and a bunch of good college players, none of whom were recruited by schools like UCLA, Louisville, Kentucky and Duke, who recruit off a base built by decades of achievements that Pitt simply does not have—not yet. And Kansas, a team whose roots go back to the man who invented basketball, and which has a collection of athletes this season that make the expectations placed on this Pitt team preposterous. But it was decreed that this Pitt team would make the Elite Eight or it would fail. And so these players have not been able to fully enjoy what should have been a magical season.

A team that generates almost no national interest, except when it loses, and whose local coverage, with a few exceptions, often teeters between the annoying and the offensive. With a *Sports Illustrated* no-article streak holding at six years, 162 wins and four Sweet Sixteens.

But here it is, still standing. And here are just a few of the 300 teams who aren't: Duke, Kentucky, Arizona, Michigan State, UConn, Syracuse, Villanova, Texas, Indiana, Wisconsin, Louisville, Marquette.

And when Pitt had to dig deep on Saturday, it was there. It may not be a perfect team, but it's a real team and it's our team:

Tyrell Biggs. It is not easy for any player to sit on the bench. It is especially difficult if you can play. Duke supposedly looked hard at Biggs. I can see why, because Pitt's fourth inside player would have been Duke's second last Thursday. When he plays, he's ready, and when he doesn't play, he cheers.

Keith Benjamin. Keith seems to be best in short bursts. But not many teams get the type of positive plays out of their eighth man that Pitt got out of Keith on Saturday. And not many players with Benjamin's explosiveness and talent are willing to accept the role he has accepted, as a junior, and as a player who played a key role on an NCAA team as a freshman.

Levance Fields. Levance is struggling lately, at both ends of the court, and at times he looks like he is worn down from a long season. But when you are the spiritual heir to Brandin Knight and Carl Krauser, you are nothing if not a fighter. As VCU found out in overtime when, in addition to his courageous three-pointer, Pitt did not commit a turnover with Levance at the helm. Fields also made a great pass to Young when Pitt went down two at the end of regulation. If it's the same situation this week, I'd like their chances with Levance on the foul line.

Sam Young. The Third Man. There have been a lot of words wasted over Young vs. Kendall. The answer is obvious, and has been. They need them both. And now, at long last, they have them. Sam is still a sophomore and at times he is still raw. But he is focused and integrated in a way that would have been hard to imagine two months ago. He is strong, he is tough, he can rebound and, best of all, he can put the ball in the basket.

Sweet Ronald Ramon. Finally, 36 games in, a moment of inspiration from the Pitt band with their European soccer chant of "Ramon, Ramon…Ramon, Raamon…" A sweet cheer for a sweet player. Fields's three-pointer in overtime was great, but Ramon's was better because Fields's was at the end of the shot clock. Ramon had a choice and never hesitated. But maybe the best thing about Ramon was the credible job he did on the very quick and dangerous Eric Maynor, especially in overtime. With about the same athletic ability, Ramon did a much better job against Maynor than Greg Paulus of Duke did, and it kept Graves off Maynor and in the game.

Mike Cook. Along with Sam Young, the most satisfying late-season development. He always has had a lot of game, but he has come a long, long way as a player, and as a Pitt player. To step up, limping, in a tight game, want to be the man at the line and then drill two foul shots, after sitting for most of a nightmarish half-hour, says a lot about Mike Cook.

Antonio Graves. Seniors first, especially this time of year. But Antonio is right here by any measure. It's time to put Antonio Graves up there with Julius Page and Jaron Brown as one of the great shut-down Pitt perimeter defenders in a shut-down era. His defense will be very hard to replace, especially since he can do a lot of good things on offense too.

Levon Kendall. My younger daughter teases me about the way I rave about Kendall. But my 82-year-old father brings a certain frame of reference to sports, having seen, for example, Babe Ruth and Lou Gehrig play in person, along with Bob Davies, a basketball player of whom most people have never heard, except those who have had occasion to visit the Hall of Fame. So it was gratifying when he turned to us at dinner on Saturday night in Buffalo and said, "I think that Kendall kid is the best all-around player on the team."

But this is Aaron Gray's team. This is the guy who came back. This is the guy who takes all of the abuse. This is the guy who fights through it. This is the guy who has bridged the gap, as Chris Taft and Carl Krauser did before him, so that Pitt is a team that has been really good for a long time, and has a chance to be really, really good for a really, really long time and not just one of those other teams that comes and goes, or comes and then goes away. Like almost all of them.

Jamie Dixon. As close as it was to a disaster, Saturday night was a triumph for Jamie. On two fundamental and related points. The first was the return on the investment of an entire season, of keeping nine players engaged, of bringing along Sam Young and Mike Cook, of having everyone understand and accept their roles, of building a team. They got contributions from just about all of them Saturday and they needed them.

But the signature moment was the start of overtime. Here is what Jamie was looking at: Gray had food poisoning. Cook was hurt. Graves and Kendall had four fouls. Fields had just missed two foul shots, either of which would have won the game. Young had missed three foul shots down the stretch. Pitt had just lost a 19-point lead. 18,000 fans were against them. VCU was electric. Looking into that huddle—and I was only about 30 feet away—I could not imagine how he could pull them together.

But he did. And they pulled each other together.

It's not the falling down. It's the getting back up.

Sweet Sixteen.

Sweet.

And I don't think they are done.

17-15

2006-2007 RECORD: 29-8

Time to let go.

That's It, Good Season   3/24/07

Alas, they were done, done in by UCLA and Ben Howland in San Jose on a night that neither team played especially well, but it was clear that, however well Pitt played, UCLA would have played a little better. It was not a memorable basketball game or a proper send-off into the cold cruel world for a group of seniors who deserved better. And then took one last kick in the nuts from the esteemed local media on the way out the door. But they will be OK. They came as boys and they are young men now.

For the rest of us, there will be another year. And then another. Until there aren't any more.

It's like the old golf saying. God gives you so many seasons. It's up to you to get 'em in.

****

Besides, my lasting memory of this week was not the game. It was something that I read in the paper and then something I saw on TV. Something that brought a sense of closure.

We all make mistakes. More than that, we all do wrong things,

things that are more than mistakes, things we regret years and decades later. At least I do, small ones and some big ones, and they bother me and some of them eat at me.

This week was a drama in two acts. The first was in a news conference leading up to the game. It was a time for happy reflection, the first game between Ben Howland and Jamie Dixon, co-architects of the Golden Era in Pitt basketball, mentor and mentee, best friends for years and years, and only playing each other as a result of the great success of each. Instead, at least as it was reported, Ben Howland took the occasion to tear into the Pittsburgh media for outing his secret courtship of the UCLA job in 2003. I choose to believe that he still was deeply bothered by how everything went down in 2003, with the best team Pitt's ever had, by far. The team that might have won everything. In my own small and perhaps delusional way, this was satisfying. If the people really affected had moved on, I hadn't, and it was good to know that maybe Ben Howland hadn't either, and that it was still eating at him.

Then, in the news conference after the game, Ben Howland broke down. Not about Jamie, as close as they are, or even about Maggie Dixon, for whom he was a pallbearer a year ago this spring. Instead it was this, and if this is not a direct quote, it's close: "You need to understand how surreal it was. Our locker rooms were right next to each other. And when I walked out, there was Brandin Knight...Brandin Knight... If it wasn't for

Brandin Knight, I wouldn't be where I am right now. Jamie wouldn't be where he is right now." And then he stopped and he paused, and he nearly broke down in tears, and he paused again, and, finally, he spoke, slowly and wistfully and from another time: "Julius Page... Jaron Brown... You have to understand... It's the players."

I do understand. I was there. We all were.

17-15

CHAPTER SEVEN

THE WINTER OF SAM

Aaron Gray was gone, to the NBA, and Levon Kendall and Antonio Graves were gone too. Still, Pitt lacked neither talent nor experience. There was a strong nucleus of three seniors: Ronald Ramon, Mike Cook and Keith Benjamin; and three juniors: Levance Fields, Sam Young and Tyrell Biggs. All had played a lot, and in big games, even if there was not much size.

These six were joined by a couple of freshmen who only played a little that season: Brad Wanamaker, a 6-2 guard from Philadelphia and Gary McGhee, a 6-10 center from Indiana; and two other freshmen who played a lot. One was Gilbert Brown, a redshirt due to illness and injury. Brown was an incredible athlete from Harrisburg, a 6-6 leaper who showed flashes at key moments of the player he is going to be.

The other was DeJuan Blair. Blair grew up 600 yards from the Peterson Events Center and had led Schenley High to the state championship. Blair was heavily recruited, although a bit less so because he had already undergone two knee surgeries and because, generously listed at 6-7 but I suspect a shade under 6-6, Blair was widely reported in the summer of 2007 to have weighed in at 302 pounds. Blair would slim down that fall to be merely enormous. Like Ontario Lett before him, DeJuan Blair played with a big smile on his face and with an uncommon agility for such a big kid. There was a lot of talk about an appropriate name. Grizzly Blair. The Blair Dunk Project. To the team, apparently, it was always The Big Fella. Or just, as we came to call out after every monstrous rebound and power dunk:

"Fella!"

First   Posted on 11/17/07

This program was built on seconds. It's a big part of what makes it so special. Part of me would just as soon watch our seconds push that boulder up the hill against the teams with the firsts. In these past seven years there have been many Pitt players who, by the time they left, would have been important players for any team in the country. But, in this entire wondrous decade, they never had recruited a pure, unadulterated first. Until now.

The thing that sets him apart is in the post. I can't do it justice. Last weekend's visiting coach, Rick Majerus, can and did:

"He has soft hands. He has good touch, and he has strong hands. He just blocked [our guys] like they were rag-dolls down there... You can't coach the three components that kid's hands have. Plus, he's got great low-body balance. Plus, he's big and strong, and he's genuinely tough. In an era where there is a lot of pretend toughness, that kid has toughness."

There have been many great players from the Pittsburgh area. Great college players. Pros. Players who developed later. A case could be made for a few more. I did not count Danny Fortson because he's not really from here. But, to me, there have only been 14 firsts in the 42 years I have watched and most of them were a long, long time ago:

Simmie Hill: Midland 1965
Norm Van Lier: Midland 1965
Kenny Durrett: Schenley 1967
Dick DeVenzio: Springdale/Ambridge 1967
Dennis Wuycik: Ambridge 1968
Billy Knight: Braddock 1970
Maurice Lucas: Schenley 1971
Ricky Coleman: Schenley 1971
Tommy Clements: Canevin 1971
Brad Davis: Monaca 1974
Sam Clancy: Fifth Avenue/Brashear 1977

This is where it gets a little bittersweet:

DeJuan Blair: Schenley 2007
Herb Pope: Aliquippa 2007
Terrelle Pryor: Jeannette 2008

All three once committed to Pitt. If Herb Pope had been Maurice Lucas instead of Simmie Hill, and if Terrelle Pryor had been Billy Knight instead of Tommy Clements, Pitt

WE ALL WE GOT

probably would have had them all. We may look back on this as a lost chance for greatness.

But I'll take the one first we have, the first one we have had, and we'll see if he can help those seconds push that boulder all the way up the hill.

17-15

238

For all of that, it was not the Winter of DeJuan Blair. It was the Winter of Sam.

The Winter of Sam

Posted on 12/8/07

There always is a defining player.
It was Brandin. Then it was Carl. Then it was Aaron.

It can be out of turn.
It was Carl when it could have been Jaron. Or Julius.

But it wasn't. It was Carl. If it ruffled any feathers, it ruffled them all the way to 31-5.

Now?

It is a good group of seniors. Good players. Leaders in their way.
Ronald Ramon, in particular, is a grown-up.
But it won't be any of them.

It could be the best player, who, make no mistake, is DeJuan Blair.
It might be the natural leader, Levance Fields.
But the defining player on this team will be Sam Young.

Sam Young is a good basketball player.
Sometimes more than good.
Sam Young does things with the basketball that are exceptional:
Score it.
Rebound it.
Attack it.

But Sam Young does not fit the mold of recent Pitt players.
Players who did things that do not come naturally to Sam:
Pass it.
Protect it.
Defend it.

Sam is a solo artist.
Not selfish.

Solo.

Not a player who does the little things.
One who does the big things.
Who is not afraid of anyone.
Some say this is what they need.
Someone who can go off-script.
Some disagree.

It doesn't matter.
Sam is who he is.
He competes.
In his way, he leads.
He is trying hard to be a Pitt player.
Without losing what makes him Sam.

How it goes will define the season.
It is the Winter of Sam.

17-15

DECEMBER 8, 2007	PITT 75 @ WASHINGTON 74
DECEMBER 15, 2007	PITT 85 OKLAHOMA STATE 68
DECEMBER 20, 2007	PITT 65 DUKE 64 (OT)
	[MADISON SQUARE GARDEN]

There are things in a life they can never take away from you, and, for Levance Fields, one of those things was the night he drove a defender past the three-point line and then stepped back and drilled a three-pointer to take down mighty Duke.

We were there that night, my wife, our younger daughter and I, a few of the 3,000 or so Pitt fans in a sea of Duke fans in Madison Square Garden, on a night when Pitt rallied from an 11-point halftime deficit, Levance and Sam Young scored Pitt's last 17 points, and DeJuan Blair announced his presence on a national stage with 15 points and 20 rebounds. Pitt held it together in overtime after Blair fouled out and, far worse, Mike Cook suffered a horrific, season-ending knee injury that ended his record as a starter in 48 straight games at 40-8.

Within a minute of Levance's shot, we received calls or text messages from our daughter in Chicago, our son in Wisconsin, my parents in Florida and my wife's parents in Pittsburgh. In our little corner of the bleachers, we had wanted a piece of Duke for a long time.

Every Freakin' Time

As 2007 comes to a close, I am proud to say that I have started nearly every day with a brisk 45-minute walk on the treadmill. Through this strict regimen, and careful diet, I have managed to gain only 15 pounds this year.

My "training" is enhanced by an iPod, a truly marvelous invention, faithfully programmed by our younger daughter. The other important element is the basement television. Lately, as our older daughter works 12 hours a day to, as she puts it, "elect a president," I watch a lot more politics. Sometimes I will watch a movie. But, more often than I'd care to admit, I will watch one of the six or seven hundred tapes that I have made of Pitt basketball and football games, other sporting events and various other things over the past 20 years. I have come to believe that there are certain things that you only can get from being at a game and certain other things that you only can get from watching the tape. For me, and, by accounts, many coaches, I really can't comment on a game "until I see the tape." Over time you have a lot of tapes.

The normal routine, then, is the iPod and the TV at the same time, both good and loud, especially since, for reasons that I cannot fathom, I am recently a bit hard of hearing in my right ear. Says I, it keeps me exercising and this is good. In the loving eyes of my wife, perhaps with some justification, there is a certain amount of excess. So, it is common for her to stop by during a showing in July of, say, the 2002 Big East Finals, to

THE WINTER OF SAM

ask something supportive like, "Did we win this time, dear?"

I have watched the Duke game several times this week. A lot of it is just to savor a very special moment in the second half, a moment that was palpable at the arena, when Pitt literally was running Duke off the floor.

I credited Duke, and still do, for gathering themselves and not getting blown out, and of course they could have won. But seeing the tape confirmed something that I felt at the time: Coach K cannot expect his guys to play tough and have them coached to fall down at the slightest hint of contact. It is not real basketball and it is one reason why many people can't stand them.

The best part of the tape is this. I explained it to my wife, who broke from tradition on this special occasion to watch this tape with me, not once, but nearly twice.

"Do you know what the best thing is?"

"No dear."

"You know how you always ask me, 'Did we win this time'"?

"Yes dear, I know."

"Do you see that shot by Levance?"

"Yes dear."

"It's gonna go in... Every freakin' time."

17-15

DECEMBER 29, 2007 | DAYTON 80 PITT 55

Coming off the high of beating Duke and the low of losing Mike Cook, Pitt already was in deep trouble at Dayton when, of all maddening things, Levance Fields backed into a Dayton cheerleader sitting courtside and broke his foot. With Fields out for 8-12 weeks and Cook gone for the year, Pitt had gone from an undefeated Top 10 team to a team entering Big East play without a single returning starter from the previous season. There was much consternation on the Board and a view, not universal but apparently held by a substantial majority, that a promising season had been lost.

I felt that this basketball program had earned more than that.

Ferdinand Foch: Posted on 12/30/07
The First Battle of the Marne.

"Hard pressed on my right. My center is yielding. Impossible to maneuver. Situation excellent. I attack."

Cheer up DT. This is Pitt f'ing basketball. It is an opportunity for greatness. They are going to make us proud.

17-15

JANUARY 2, 2008	PITT 96 LAFAYETTE 75
JANUARY 6, 2008	VILLANOVA 64 PITT 63

So it began. The road that Pitt had in front of it included six other Big East teams that would finish the season in the Top 25. At times it seemed like they were traveling this road in the Joad family wagon in The Grapes of Wrath. *No depth. No height. No point guard. The sense that, wherever they were going, they had to stay together to get there.*

Detour   Posted on 1/6/08

When we drive home to Pittsburgh from my sister's in Boston, there always is a choice. We can take Route 80 to I-79. It usually is smooth sailing all the way, and it almost always turns out to be a pretty good trip.

There is another way to go, though. You can cut down Route 28. It is about 80 miles long. The first 40 miles is slow going, with a lot of stops and starts. It's a winding road, two lanes, and at night it can be delicate. There are a few small towns where it is traffic light by traffic light. Sometimes you feel like you are not getting anywhere at all.

Pitt turned off onto Route 28 this week. It will not be a smooth ride.

Today, they got some really encouraging play, even if it was not quite enough. To strain the metaphor, Sam Young is capable of veering off the road but today he had both hands on the wheel. Sam can score, and that's important, but he did more than that. He played defense. He hit the boards. Struggling all year with a 1 to 4 assist to turnover ratio, he found Keith Benjamin with a perfect pass in rhythm for an uncontested three. He also demonstrated a lost art of basketball, with several exquisite left-handed moves to the basket.

DeJuan Blair is an 18-wheeler, and you do not want to be in his lane. Even as he made big plays at the end, though, plays that almost won the game, he also showed that he has things to learn and that he would be better at 25-30 minutes than at 37. There are probably 15 teams that could be Final Four contenders with DeJuan Blair. If they can get down Route 28, Pitt could be one of them.

Gilbert Brown is a sports car, maybe a Porsche. The best thing about Gilbert Brown is that, for such a great athlete, he plays under control and in the flow and he has a good feel for the game. He needs to get a little stronger and hit the defensive boards harder. I don't love his stroke the way some others do. He needs to put it on the floor with more confidence. Sometimes he stands up too straight on defense, although his lateral quickness is exceptional. So he has plenty to work on and it will take time. But he is going to be great. Not good. Great.

[I interrupt this post to tell you about a weird dream I had today. I dreamed that I was watching a Pitt game and that

THE WINTER OF SAM

Keith Benjamin was playing point guard and not too badly. Then, he returned to shooting guard and small forward and made some of the plays I had seen him make in short bursts for Pitt when I was not dreaming, only more of them, more like what I had seen in the summer league, including a simply gorgeous high bank shot from the left of the key that was vintage John Wooden UCLA.]

On Route 28, one thing you need to be careful about is to have enough gas. There are wide stretches where you would not want to be caught short. Jamie says Pitt was not too tired today. I probably don't agree. Either way, as hard as this team plays, they cannot play an 18-game Big East season with barely more than six players. So they need to live with Brad Wanamaker's growing pains a little more than they did today.

It's only fair to Sweet Ronald Ramon.

Ronald may be a Yugo, as it goes. He had a rough game today and lately he has had a few of them. He is small and he is slow and he can't dribble. But he is a basketball player and he is a Pitt basketball player and he is one of my favorite Pitt basketball players. He is playing out his senior year at a position that is not his best and where he will be overmatched at times because, my Keith Benjamin dreams notwithstanding, there simply is nobody else.

Ronald Ramon is doing all this with a bad shoulder that was partly dislocated last week. I am reminded of something that

Myron Cope once said about Mario Lemieux: "I have talked to a lot of doctors and I have never had one of them tell me that what you should do for a bad back is play some hockey." I would be surprised if any doctor would suggest that what Ronald Ramon should do for his shoulder is play point guard against a full court press for 31 minutes. That's what he did today and that's what he will keep doing for as long as his shoulder holds up, maybe successfully and sometimes maybe not, and sometimes he will look bad. But he will keep playing, because that's what they need and that's the kind of teammate he is and that's the kind of kid he is.

Today, all of that added up to one play short. It was a proud performance and if they play that way 18 times and go 0-18, it will be a proud season. But they won't. As they showed today against a good team in a tough gym, this Pitt team still is plenty good. They just need to get back on Route 28, and we need to be ready for all the stops and starts along the way.

Why do people go down Route 28 anyway, when they could stay on the smooth roads, on Route 80 and then I-79? Because it's the best way to go. When you hit Kittanning you start to fly and it's only 40 miles in. Today made one thing clear: if they can get through all the stops and starts and the little towns along the way, if they can hang together and then get Levance Fields back, really back, by the time they hit Kittanning, this Pitt team could be flying all the way home.

17-15

| JANUARY 9, 2008 | PITT 79 @ SOUTH FLORIDA 66 |
| JANUARY 12, 2008 | PITT 84 SETON HALL 70 |

Led by a couple of players who had risen to meet the crisis, Pitt held firm in good wins over a couple of second-division teams. Next was defending champion and pre-season favorite Georgetown, the team that had blown them out of the Big East finals.

Growin' Up   Posted on 1/13/08

It has been a very good week for our Pitt Panthers and it is about to get better because Pitt is going to take down Georgetown tomorrow night.

There is much to report. Contributions abound, from Ramon to Brown to even the freshmen subs, McGhee and Wanamaker. Then there is DeJuan Blair. "A monster. A beast," says Seton Hall Coach Bobby Gonzalez. But, most of all, two players who have been at the center of Pitt's holding it together in a crisis, two players who are growing up.

The Winter of Sam is going very well. Someday, hopefully, Sam will have the last laugh, and among the things he will laugh about are some of the things that make him Sam, including, yesterday, another old favorite from last year, going to take the ball out of bounds while his teammates were setting up to play defense 60 feet away.

Even as I am starting to view these things with a bemused fondness, I know that they are only some of the things that make him Sam. When I think of Sam, I think of something else, something I used to do a long time ago to no good effect, but which is a part of me to this day: in a gym, by myself, just bouncing the ball and shooting and making moves and dreaming about playing basketball. While any benefits that I ever got were spiritual, Sam Young has come out of that gym with a vastly expanded game: a slashing game, a post game, a put-back game, a pull-up game and most striking, a jumper that he's earned the right to shoot. Best of all, day by day, Sam has something else: a team game.

Sam Young has thrown more good passes in the past two weeks than he did his first two years. As he comes to trust that all of the things he has worked so hard on will be used in the flow, he is starting to let them come in the flow. On defense, he is still too flat-footed and he does not help cover for others as much he could. But he is better than he was. Since the injuries, Sam has been a good leader, including, importantly, in defeat.

I felt that the Winter of Sam could go either way. So far it is going the right way. Sam Young is growing up, he is becoming a terrific basketball player and he played two fantastic basketball games this week.

If the rise of Sam Young is heartening, the rise of Keith Benjamin is shocking. Keith Benjamin has been a productive player at Pitt for three years. People forget that Keith Benjamin played a key role as a freshman, including in the 2005 NCAA Tournament. A year later, he was a starter at the end on a very fine team and when he missed the NCAAs with what they feared was meningitis, it was a big loss. Keith always has been capable of the highlight play. If you picked the most electrifying plays of the past seven years, Keith's two-handed slam over Syracuse his sophomore year would be near the top of the list. More than that, there can be an artistic quality to the way Keith Benjamin plays basketball. His pull-up jumper when he hangs in the air is a thing of beauty, even more so when he uses the glass. On those occasions when he pulls down a two-handed rebound in traffic he is reminiscent of some of the great 6-2 leaping forwards, players like Ollie Taylor and Waymon Britt.

But somewhere along the way it seemed like Keith just stalled out. Yes, he was productive, but in short spurts. Sometimes he was not instinctive and lost concentration. He did not move the ball as well as some others. In the rich Pitt tradition of "seconds" he was a two and a half. Not quite skilled enough for shooting guard, not quite big enough for small forward. Anyone who saw him play in the summer league had to wonder if he had gone to the wrong school, that he was born for the open court and not the half court. A decent player, but a career reserve. A player, but not a Player.

Or so it seemed. But Keith Benjamin loves basketball too and while others may have given up on him ever being more than that, he never gave up on himself. Like Sam, he found comfort in that gym and he came out of it a more confident player with a more consistent shot. When he finally got the chance, he seized it. Keith Benjamin already has earned the right to call himself a college basketball player. Now he has a chance to be remembered, and remember himself, as something more.

Keith Benjamin. Player.

Pitt is growing up. With, by the way, a coach who is growing by the game. It has already been a memorable season and it is about to get more memorable tomorrow night.

17-15

JANUARY 14, 2008	PITT 69 GEORGETOWN 60
JANUARY 19, 2008	CINCINNATI 62 PITT 59
JANUARY 23, 2008	PITT 81 @ ST. JOHN'S 57
JANUARY 26, 2008	RUTGERS 77 PITT 64
JANUARY 30, 2008	PITT 69 VILLANOVA 57
FEBRUARY 2, 2008	UCONN 60 PITT 53
FEBRUARY 7, 2008	PITT 55 WVU 54

Georgetown lost only six games all season. One was to a depleted Pitt team on a night when Keith Benjamin and Ronald Ramon each scored 18 points and DeJuan Blair outplayed Georgetown's 7-2 All-American Roy Hibbert, with 15 points and 9 rebounds. After the huge win over Georgetown it was up and down for awhile, including another injury, a nasty six-stitch cut to Keith Benjamin's shooting hand that would last a month, and a startling second-half collapse at home against 15th-place Rutgers.

Pitt rebounded with a nice win over a Villanova team that would make the Sweet 16, and a strong effort on the road against a good UConn team that still is not quite UCONN but will be soon. Pitt then struggled at home against a tough West Virginia team that also would reach the Sweet 16. But when Keith Benjamin found Ronald Ramon in the left corner with eight tenths of a second to go, ten minutes later we were all on SportsCenter.

Sweet Ronald Ramon

There is just something about a pure jump shooter. It is as though the good Lord says: "I would like the world to stop for a moment. Ronald Ramon will be shooting his jump shot now." A pure jump shooter lives on in basketball memory when better athletes are long forgotten. Brian Magid. Joey Sonar Hassett. In the mid-1990s, Arkansas had a little guard named Alex Dillard. His stroke was maybe not quite as pure but he would launch it from 30 feet and my six-year-old son and I would scream out: "He's a BOMBER!"

I have seen many pure jump shots by Sweet Ronald Ramon and three memorable ones. The first was against Notre Dame his sophomore year when he hit a bomb from the deep right corner after it appeared that another classic shooter, Chris Quinn, would lead Notre Dame to a remarkable comeback win. The second was in overtime against Virginia Commonwealth in Buffalo last March, from the same right corner; again it was key in thwarting an epic comeback. The third, of course, was on Thursday night. It was from the left corner this time but just as true. And just as clutch. It also is a shot that I will never forget because I was about three feet away from Ronald Ramon when he shot it.

Over the years, Pitt has had many clutch players who have hit many big shots. Of all the Pitt players I have seen, if the game was on the line and they got one open look at a long jumper, I would put my money on Sweet Ronald Ramon.

17-15

FEBRUARY 12, 2008	PITT 82 PROVIDENCE 63
FEBRUARY 15, 2008	MARQUETTE 72 PITT 54
FEBRUARY 21, 2008	NOTRE DAME 82 PITT 70

Having held together for a month and a half without Levance Fields, Pitt promptly collapsed upon his return, at Marquette, a game we attended with our son, his cousin, a good friend from long ago, and his wife, all down from Madison. Then, on to see our daughter in Chicago. A great trip, save one miserable basketball game.

Second Wind   Posted on 2/23/08

For the first time in seven years, Pitt looks like a tired team. They either will get their second wind or they won't.

Marquette was a train wreck. But the game that really is of concern is Notre Dame, because it was not a train wreck. For thirty minutes or so, Pitt played passionately and well. There has been much written and said about why they fell apart in the last ten minutes. To me it was clear as a bell. Pitt simply hit the wall. Not because they weren't trying. Because it just wasn't there. Watching Notre Dame manhandle Pitt down the stretch reminded me of what Pitt has done to so many teams the past seven years. It was painful to watch it go the other way.

There are reasons. In the best of times, this is the grinding part of a long season, and these are far from the best of times.

Mike Cook is gone. Levance is back, but we knew it would take time for him to get back up to game speed. A team that has not been able to have real practices.

Whatever the reasons, at least for the moment, Pitt looks like just another team running up and down the court. For six and a half years, you could watch a Pitt game on TV from across a crowded room and know it was Pitt. All the talk of go-to guys, up tempo and blue chip recruits that is a staple of this Board goes in one ear and out the other for me. I want to see a team that screws its navel into the ground on defense, especially when they need big stops. I want to see the extra pass, of which Marquette threw five to every one for Pitt, and which led to most of the Notre Dame threes down the stretch. I want to see a team that pounds the boards. I want to see a team that dictates tempo and cannot be sped up.

I want to see Pitt basketball.

17-15

FEBRUARY 24, 2008	LOUISVILLE 75 PITT 73
FEBRUARY 27, 2008	PITT 73 CINCINNATI 67
MARCH 1, 2008	PITT 82 @ SYRACUSE 77

The offense was improving as Levance Fields got healthier and started to run the show, but Pitt still could not guard anyone and they also were having trouble on the boards.

Pitt trailed Syracuse 75-64 with 3:37 to play and a once-promising season that they had held together through a crisis appeared to be getting away from them. Then Pitt finished the game with a startling 18-2 run.

March

Posted on 3/1/08

This could be the shot of adrenaline they need and at just the right time. It was a little fluky today. To a point, Syracuse lost it as much as Pitt won it.

But there was more to it than that. Levance Fields hit eight straight foul shots. After going, literally, 0 for February from three, Gilbert Brown hit two huge three-pointers at the end. Ronald Ramon had a crucial steal and finish. Fields's rebound and DeJuan Blair's block were critical. And Sam Young made a steal they will be showing for years and years, with a perfect over-the-shoulder pass leading to the final points of a brilliant and fiercely determined performance by Keith Benjamin.

A coach who would not let them give up.

It may just be another special regular season memory in a season full of them, but one in which that will be our portion. This team is simply awful defensively of late. It may be a pipe dream to think it can get better enough fast enough for them to make some noise.

Pitt did gain some ground on one of their big recent problems, out-rebounding a big, strong, Syracuse team, including 11-4 on the offensive boards. Of course, that's because Syracuse never missed. Pitt has major problems with both individual and team defense. Anyone on this Board who ever uttered a critical word about Antonio Graves and Levon Kendall last year might consider a note of penance.

And yet.

Here are a couple straws to grasp. Part of it is transition defense. That can be corrected. On the biggest issue, help defense, they look so confused that it gives you the feeling that they could get a lot better. So the scenario is this. Play WVU on spirit on Monday night. More than a week to go to school on defense before the Big East Tournament, interrupted only by a dry run against a DePaul team that Pitt should beat. Then, who knows.

It is March. The cruelest month. The month where teams go to die. But also, as ever, the Month of Dreams.

17-15

MARCH 3, 2008	WEST VIRGINIA 76 PITT 62
MARCH 9, 2008	PITT 98 DEPAUL 79
MARCH 12, 2008	PITT 70 CINCINNATI 64
	[BIG EAST TOURNAMENT]

If beauty is truth, and truth beauty, some of the beauty here is by design obscured. These are young people and they are doing what they can. There is no profound purpose in running them down.

But what previously had been hinted now can be said: my son had Carl and I had Sam, and to understand how proud I was of Sam Young during the 2008 Big East Basketball Tournament, you would need to understand how he had worn me out for the better part of the preceding three years.

Anyone who knows me knows how hard it is for me to admit when I am wrong. I was wrong about Sam Young. About what he was capable of as a player. About what he was capable of as a leader.

The Enigma Machine   Posted on 3/13/2008

But when he really comes to play at both ends of the court…

In August 1975, a good friend of mine and I drove to Boston to drop off some furniture at my sister's third-floor college apartment, no small task, for which we were rewarded by my parents with a couple days in Cape Cod. When we finally crashed at the hotel on Sunday night we had been up for almost two days. Before drifting off, we put on *60 Minutes,* and what we saw that night we still talk about to this day.

The segment was called "The Enigma Machine." It was about the encryption machine the Nazis used in World War II and how the best mathematicians, puzzle solvers and code breakers on the Allied side broke the code, intercepted crucial messages, won the war, and saved the world. Among the key members of the team was William Bundy, the brother of the more well-known McGeorge Bundy, who was cited less favorably by the late journalist and noted basketball writer, David Halberstam, in *The Best and the Brightest,* an analysis of how the best minds of a generation managed to steer the country into a quagmire in Vietnam.

It would take the Enigma Machine to figure out Sam Young. I know I can't.

But when he really comes to play at both ends of the court. When he understands that a point allowed counts as much as a point scored. That many possessions only end with a defensive rebound. Or a huge block. Or three of them in the last three minutes. When he understands that an assist not only counts for points but gets everyone else involved. When he puts his arm around Levance after a rough play, the way he did a couple weeks ago with Gary McGhee.

There were many other important performances tonight,

most notably by the seniors, Keith Benjamin and Ronald Ramon, and a timely and improved effort on the boards by Tyrell Biggs. But Sam Young set the tone from the jump with his defense on a fine player, Williamson, who scored 27 two weeks ago and eight tonight. Then he saved them at the end and he did it with defense. All on a night when his running mate in the post was playing like the freshman he is.

If Sam Young can continue to unlock the player that is in him, if his coaches can continue to help him unlock the player that is in him, on both ends of the court and on the boards, then Pitt will have a special player.

Whatever else happens, Pitt had a special player tonight.

17-15

| MARCH 13, 2008 | PITT 76 LOUISVILLE 69 (OT) |
| | [BIG EAST TOURNAMENT] |

A classic basketball game. One of the best wins in the past seven years, against a Louisville team that would make the Elite Eight and finish Number 6 in the country. A team that in truth may have been a little better than Pitt. A team that was fresher. With a coach, Rick Pitino, who had won a national championship and taken three different schools to the Final Four, but who had been knocked out of the Big East Tournament by Pitt and Jamie Dixon in each of the previous two seasons. Now it was three.

Louisville wanted it badly. Pitt wanted it more.

Snap Double   Posted on 3/14/08

As my oldest daughter taught me, it's not the electric guitar or the drums. It's the bass, and if it's great, you feel it right in your gut.

You don't need anyone to tell you when you are watching a great basketball game. You feel it right in your gut.

The quiet pride of Sweet Ronald Ramon. The renewed and redoubled effort of Tyrell Biggs. The toughness of DeJuan Blair, the next great Schenley High School player, as he stood up to Louisville's big and talented front line on the same court where 37 years ago next week, I saw the first great Schenley

High School player, Kenny Durrett, play for LaSalle. Let's not leave out the valiant effort of Louisville and especially a terrific young player in Earl Clark.

On a night when their hopes and dreams once again became my hopes and dreams, three things stood out most of all:

1. Levance Fields. One of my out-of-town guests, someone who knows his basketball, did not love Levance's game or, for that matter, Pitt's offense. Dribbles too much. What's with the funky fall back jumper? Fair points, if you don't know the whole story. I told him the long version, that Levance means everything to this team, that with him everyone is in the right spot, that it was night and day how the offense ran when he came back, and now the defense is back too. Or I could have given him the short version:

35 minutes of intense, full-court pressure.
6 assists. 1 turnover.

2. S. Young. F 40 8-19 0-4 5-7 5 12 4 2 3 2 3 21

21 points. 12 rebounds. *4 assists.* 3 steals. 2 blocks.
1 leader.

Yes.

YES.

YES!!!

3. Gilbert Brown. Gilbert the Gazelle. When he was setting up the block from half court I just said to my friend, "Watch this." Gilbert Brown had two crucial three-pointers down the stretch against Syracuse. If it were up to me, he would not take another the rest of the year. It is not what he does, not yet. What he does is slash and pull up, move the ball and finish once in a while, and, while nobody has been watching, in the past three weeks he has started to hit the boards, with eight huge ones tonight.

There is one more thing, though, maybe the biggest thing, which would make four things, and Gilbert Brown was in the middle of it, too:

4. The Ben Howland Snap Double. If you go back to March 2001, when Pitt lit the fuse on what is now a 17-6 run in the Big East Tournament, you will see Isaac Hawkins putting the Ben Howland Snap Double on Troy Murphy. A fast, aggressive, decisive double team in the post. The same one Ben Howland had Luc Richard Mbah a Moute put on Aaron Gray last year. The same one that Sam Young put on David Padgett tonight. But there was a twist tonight. David Padgett is a very fine player, and an excellent passer. So, time after time, especially down the stretch, Padgett would see the Snap Double and he would make the right pass, the cross-court pass to the wing. The twist was that Gilbert Brown was so quick, so good laterally, that Louisville almost never even got

WE ALL WE GOT

off a three-pointer, much less a good look, even after they switched from Terrence Williams to their best shooter, Jerry Smith. Which is why Gilbert Brown was not coming out of that game, even if that meant keeping Keith Benjamin on the bench.

So let's call it the Ben Howland Snap Double with a Gilbert Brown Twist. Or we could call it by its correct name:

The Jamie Dixon Snap Double.

17-15

| MARCH 14, 2008 | PITT 68 MARQUETTE 61 |
| | [BIG EAST TOURNAMENT] |

For the second year in a row, Pitt avenged a late-season loss at Marquette with a win in the Big East Tournament. Sam Young with 22 points had his third straight 20-point game, supported by 14 points from Ronald Ramon, another strong floor game by Levance Fields and 8 important rebounds off the bench by the renewed Tyrell Biggs.

Team of the Decade   Posted on 3/15/08

Pitt has won only one Big East Tournament championship. In the basketball world, let alone the world at large, it is of little note. Yet for those of us who have seen it, who have been here, who in a vicarious but real way have lived it, watching Pitt make seven Big East finals in eight years is almost indescribable:

2001	2002	2003
Miami	Boston College	Providence
Notre Dame	Miami	Boston College
Syracuse		UConn

2004	2006	2007
Virginia Tech	Louisville	Marquette
Boston College	West Virginia	Louisville
	Villanova	

2008

Cincinnati
Louisville
Marquette

These are the teams that Pitt has beaten in this tournament the past eight years. Almost all of them have been good. Most have been very good. Several have been great.

There have been other excellent Big East teams in this decade, teams that have had great runs, national championship teams, teams that have been better than Pitt at times. Boston College, Georgetown, Syracuse, West Virginia. Most of all, UConn. But no team in the Big East in this decade has had the sustained excellence that Pitt has had.

Georgetown looks big, strong, deep and fresh. Pitt looked exhausted in the last 23 minutes tonight. If I have learned nothing else, though, I have learned not to underestimate the 2007-2008 Pitt basketball team. The seventh Pitt basketball team in eight years to reach the finals of the Big East Tournament. And, I predict, somehow, some way, against all odds and all reason, the winner of the 2008 Big East Tournament, with a claim to be the Team of the Decade in the Big East Conference.

17-15

MARCH 15, 2008	PITT 74 GEORGETOWN 65
	[BIG EAST FINALS]

No team in the history of the Big East playing its fourth game had won the tournament against a team playing its third. In the tradition of 2003, Pitt had five players in double figures and important contributions from every player. Sam Young had 16 points and three blocks and was the Most Valuable Player. Levance Fields was All-Tournament; Ronald Ramon scored 17 and also should have been. DeJuan Blair had 10 and 10. Gilbert Brown had 12 points, including two key three-pointers I had urged him not to shoot. Keith Benjamin and Tyrell Biggs combined for 10 rebounds. Life was almost perfect, again.

Champions   Posted on 3/16/08

Keith Benjamin	Jamie Dixon
Tyrell Biggs	Tom Herrion
DeJuan Blair	Patrick Sandle
Gilbert Brown	Orlando Antigua
Mike Cook	Brandin Knight
Cassin Diggs	Brian Regan
Levance Fields	Tony Salesi
Tim Frye	Tim Beltz
Gary McGhee	
Maurice Polen	
Ronald Ramon	
Brad Wanamaker	
Sam Young	
Austin Wallace	

The 2008 Big East Conference Tournament Champions.

For the rest of their lives, these young men will remember
four nights in March 2008.

What they accomplished. What they overcame.
What they learned from the people who believed in them.
What they meant to each other.
When they were a team in the truest sense.
When they played basketball the way it was meant to be played.
When they played it as hard as it can be played.

17-15

MARCH 20, 2008	PITT 82 ORAL ROBERTS 63
	[NCAA TOURNAMENT]
MARCH 22, 2008	MICHIGAN STATE 65 PITT 54
	[NCAA TOURNAMENT]

2007-2008 RECORD: 27-10.

It might be nice to finish this book with an NCAA Championship. That's how sports stories end. Of course, that really wouldn't be the end.

Every team gets its own journey. And every person.

That's It, Good Season   Posted on 3/25/08

The reason I stayed up all night on Friday to catch a 5:40 a.m. flight to Denver was to see two talented and mentally tough teams play in the NCAA basketball tournament. The reason my wife went with me is that she loves me.

We both knew there was a good chance that this would be the last time we would get to see this Pitt basketball team. Like Pitt, Michigan State is a top of the line team with a top of the line coach, and they were just a little better than Pitt on Saturday night. Whether they would have been better than Pitt last week or next week, who knows, but they were better on Saturday night. Michigan State is not a team that you want to play on a night when you don't bring your best game. They play hard and clean, and they are fundamentally sound and nothing comes easy against them.

For whatever reason, Pitt was not quite at their best on Saturday night. Before the Marquette game in New York, the level of enthusiasm in the Pitt huddle was strikingly higher, and Pitt jumped out to a big lead in that game. In Denver on Saturday night, that spark just seemed to be missing, even before the game. Pitt has played a lot of big, emotional games in the past two weeks and it is hard to keep that fine edge.

So this was the end of the line for another special team in a very special time in Pitt basketball. Pitt has now averaged 27 wins for seven seasons. This team won its 27 games without, in truth, a single starter who stood even 6-6, and only two who stood even 6-2. This team won its 27 games playing over half the Big East season with four freshmen among its top eight players. This team won its 27 games playing most of the season without a key senior leader, much of the season without its point guard and without a single starter from last season, and some of the season without enough players to hold a real practice.

Most of all, this team won its 27 games with five magical nights in New York City; one in December against Duke and four in March in a Big East Championship rampage over Cincinnati, Louisville, Marquette and Georgetown that will be its moment forever.

Some people will say that this was another Pitt team that came up short in the NCAA Tournament. It is a subject of modest interest to me, at most. But, regardless, with what it had, all this team went through and what it accomplished, to say that this team came up short in any way other than stature is just silly.

In the great circle of life it is time to say goodbye. To the seniors:

Mike Cook. A brief personal story. In early January, our son had shoulder surgery at UPMC Southside. Although it was routine as surgeries go, any parent who has had a child go through any surgery knows that the imagination races as you wait for the call to come to the recovery room. So it was that we sat three feet away from Mike Cook's family for two hours that day until my wife realized who they were, and that they had been waiting even longer for the results of a complicated and serious knee surgery. We briefly wished them well, not wanting to intrude and focused on our own thoughts. Thankfully, it appears a few months later that both our son and theirs are on the road to recovery. Cheering for Mike Cook in New York, seeing him get hurt so badly that night and then seeing his family that day reinforced what we all should remember but sometimes don't: that these are kids, with families and lives and concerns far beyond basketball.

Mike Cook the basketball player was an important contributor to this team and a great loss. As the season went on, it became very clear that Mike Cook the teammate, leader and friend remained a very big part of this team. Mike Cook came to Pitt as a star. He left as something even better.

Mike Cook: Team Player.

Keith Benjamin. This was a proud season for Keith Benjamin. Years ago Johnny Majors used to talk about the time when players needed to come to the front. When Cook and then Fields were injured, and the season was on the line, Keith Benjamin came to the front. That has been well-chronicled and it will be why Pitt fans always will fondly remember Keith Benjamin. I would add two other points. Keith Benjamin came a long way this year as a vocal leader and public spokesman for the team. He also was a big part of pulling Pitt out of the second crisis of its season, when the defense inexplicably went away.

Keith Benjamin: Senior Leader.

Ronald Ramon. When I first saw Ronald Ramon play basketball, at an all-star game at the Pete in April 2004, I posted a run-down of his strengths and limitations. Looking back, the most important part was this: "B Man says that he's a player who really grows on you." Ronald Ramon has grown on me and many other Pitt fans for four years. He has been a part of what they are for so long that it is hard to imagine that he won't be there next year. It will be hard not to see the jump shot that is a small work of art. It will be hard not to see the hundred little ways that he would help them win.

There was something fitting, even if sad, about Ronald Ramon going out on a tough shooting night. One thing I think of when I think of Ronald Ramon is perspective. I don't know him but I would bet that Ronald Ramon has a good perspective on being a college basketball player. That if you play it all out, as Ronald Ramon did for four years, you are going to have your great days and your rough days and lots of other kinds of days. Ronald Ramon played big—huge in fact—in many, many important games, and he always showed up, including on Saturday. For some Pitt players over the years, I have worried about what will become of them when they don't have basketball anymore. Ronald Ramon is not one of them.

Ronald Ramon: Grown-up.

And, one last time:

Sweet Ronald Ramon.

Mike Cook, Keith Benjamin and Ronald Ramon are part of the Golden Era of Pitt basketball and always will be. They have helped to form the foundation of the next special Pitt basketball team, the 2008-2009 team, a team that might be extra-special.

That story remains to be written. We have been reminded this season that nothing in life is certain. But whatever else, the 2008-2009 team, and all Pitt basketball teams from now on, will have the honor and the responsibility of playing Pitt basketball, for a program built from almost nothing into one of the best college basketball programs in the country. Built with passion and determination and hope, and with an almost irrational belief in what is possible.

17-15

EPILOGUE

We hold on to our triumphs, great and small, along with our failures. In 1977, when I was 20 years old, I worked as a counselor at a summer camp in West Virginia. It was a very sweet and important time in my life and, as it turned out, basketball was at the center of it.

There was a counselor basketball league, the KBA, and it was a big deal at our little camp in the summer of 1977. It wasn't exactly the Big Five at the Palestra but we did draw a record crowd of 71 for a doubleheader one afternoon during general swim. The level of play was, to be kind, low. In that tiny pond, I was one of the better players, possibly even as good as our lone girl player, known, fondly, as "Merle the Pearl."

In fact, I was the captain of the championship team, the San Andreas Fault. 14-2, I'll have you know. Our star center, the assistant maintenance man at the camp, was 6-3 and aggressive and loud and fun and a very good player by our modest standards. We surrounded him with the biggest guys we could find, whether they could play basketball or not, including a 36-year-old who was 6-6 and reminiscent of Chief Broom in *One Flew over the Cuckoo's Nest*. We had a plodding bear of a power forward who used to announce the games as he ran down the court and later was a referee in the Israeli professional league. Our shooting guard, a close friend to this day, stood in the corner firing errant left-handed set shots and, then as now, spouting errant right-wing politics. It was the era of the Steelers-Raiders rivalry, a dispute that actually ended up in a courtroom, as crazy as that sounds. We were known as "The Criminal Element" from that trial, although as the old joke goes, as a Jewish street gang we didn't fight, we litigated. We were generally viewed as a bunch of loudmouths because, well, that's what we were.

In our blustering way, we won the championship. I won something else, though, and it was much more important. I am a point guard in the game of life, and my job on that team and any other one I ever played on was to pass the ball. I surely could not shoot it. One of the girl counselors in another unit later told me that I seemed like the biggest jerk of all. It was no small accomplishment to get even one vote for that award, and I got many. But she noticed that I passed the ball and she thought that there might be some good in me.

The next summer we worked in the same unit and came to realize that we both loved children and watching them grow up. We have three of them now, the three best in the whole world as luck would have it, and we have been married 25 years this past summer. We still love watching children grow up, our own and our Pitt Panthers too.

I never was a real player, but I loved to play. And everything good that has happened in my life in the past 30 years has come at least in part from basketball. It's a team game.

ACKNOWLEDGEMENTS

This book has been a labor of love, written at a time of life when, like many people my age, I was looking for a different kind of satisfaction. For me, a big part of this satisfaction was the invaluable help I received from family and friends along the way.

To my family for tolerating this project to the point that I could take it as encouragement: my wife Andee for her unflagging moral support and careful edits and our children Lauren, Rachel and David for their inspiration.

To my friends at the University of Pittsburgh, including Jerry Cochran, Steve Pederson, Jamie Dixon, E.J. Borghetti and Alan Garfinkel, each of whom provided critical guidance and assistance. Special thanks to E.J. and Greg Hotchkiss for providing spectacular photographs. Most of all, to Chancellor Mark Nordenberg for his encouragement and support throughout the project, and for somehow making time that I know he did not have to write a foreword that captured a unique perspective on the progress of the Pitt basketball program and its importance to the University community.

To my "readers" and sounding boards, both the pros—Kevin Gorman and Alan Paul—and the people who, like me, were not pros—Jim Whalen, Alan London, Doug Cameron, Larry Flatley, Natalie and Kenn Moritz, Jeremy Feinstein, Fred Colen, Jim Doerfler, Pat Gentile, Jeff Mishkin, Gary Simon,

Mark Lowenthal, Rick and David Kaufman, the Berez family and my parents, Amy and Frank Lowenstein, each of whom added immeasurably to this book in different ways. And to Rick Kaufman and my other Duke grad friends, a note of thanks for your graciousness and an apology for my failure to rise above that small-minded obsession.

To my friends at Word Association—Tom Costello, Theresa Doerfler and Gina Datres—for their guidance and professionalism in editing and publishing this book. In my field—commercial litigation—I am accustomed to learning enough about a business to be dangerous. I am confident that Tom, Theresa and Gina now consider me dangerous on the subject of book publishing. I am particularly indebted to Theresa Doerfler for her patient and persistent editing, which assured that this book would not be finished until it was as good as we could make it.

To all of the people with whom we go to the games, and to the Big East Tournament and the NCAAs, and who make basketball a shared experience for us.

To my "imaginary friends" on the Pantherlair message board on Rivals.com, whoever you are, for your many years of insights and good company.

And, finally, to the Pitt basketball teams of 2002 through 2008 for giving all of us a chance to watch a team play basketball the right way.

CHAPTER PHOTOS

OPENING PHOTO
Levance Fields takes down Duke

CHAPTER 1
Brandin Knight

CHAPTER 2
2003 Big East Finals

CHAPTER 3
Torrie Morris
Jaron Brown
Julius Page

CHAPTER 4
Chevy Troutman

CHAPTER 5
Carl Krauser

CHAPTER 6
Aaron Gray

CHAPTER 7
Sam Young